Writing Public Policy

A Practical Guide to Communicating in the Policy Making Process

SECOND EDITION

Catherine F. Smith
East Carolina University

OXFORD
UNIVERSITY PRESS
2010

Oxford University Press, Inc., publishes works that further
Oxford University's objective of excellence
in research, scholarship, and education.

Oxford New York
Auckland Cape Town Dar es Salaam Hong Kong Karachi
Kuala Lumpur Madrid Melbourne Mexico City Nairobi
New Delhi Shanghai Taipei Toronto

With offices in
Argentina Austria Brazil Chile Czech Republic France Greece
Guatemala Hungary Italy Japan Poland Portugal Singapore
South Korea Switzerland Thailand Turkey Ukraine Vietnam

Published by Oxford University Press, Inc.
198 Madison Avenue, New York, New York 10016
http://www.oup.com

Library of Congress Cataloging-in-Publication Data

Smith, Catherine F. (Catherine Findley), 1942–
    Writing public policy : a practical guide to communicating in
the policy making process / Catherine F. Smith.—2nd ed.
        p. cm.
    Includes bibliographical references and index.
    ISBN 978-0-19-537982-2
    1. Communication in public administration.   2. Written communication.
I. Title.
    JF1525.C59S64   2009
    320.6—dc22   2009008661

9 8 7 6 5 4 3 2 1

Printed in the United States of America
on acid-free paper

To John, best friend and best critic

Contents

Preface

A student returning to campus from a summer internship in a Washington, D.C., public policy think tank said this about the lesson she learned: "In public policy work, if you can't write it or say it, you can't do it."

Public policy professionals will recognize the truth of the observation. As an experienced writing teacher and as a communications consultant in government and nongovernmental organizations, I recognize it, too. Consequently, I wrote this book to prepare students, professionals, and active citizens to "do" public policy work by writing (and speaking) effectively in democratic public processes.

What Is the Purpose of This Book?

This practical guide aims to develop communication know-how and skill. Know-how means understanding what to do or having situational and contextual awareness. Skill means knowing how to do or having ready competencies.

This guide

- describes the public policy making process,
- identifies communication's functions and limitations in that process,
- explains standards and expectations for communicating in the public sector,

- offers guided practice in selected public policy communication genres.

It does not

- discuss theory of public policy, writing, or communication,
- teach introductory policy analysis, public administration, written composition, or public speaking.

What Is This Book About?

Public policy making in a democracy is an institutional process of solving problems that affect society or its environment. Communication is integral to the process.

Policy making includes the following activities:

- Defining the problem
- Developing knowledge including knowledge of prior action or inaction on the problem
- Proposing policy alternatives
- Deliberating the alternatives
- Adopting policy
- Administering and implementing policy
- Changing policy

Actual processes are not as linear as this list suggests. Rather, these are the expected phases of a policy cycle. They do not always occur in order, or in a single pass, or in a simple way. Actual policy making is recursive and messy.

Not shown on the list are the communications on which the phases of policy making rely. For example, problem definition might require any or all of the following documents or interactions: notes by participants on personal experiences with problematic conditions, an expert briefing for an elected official on the problematic conditions, a position paper framing the problem presented by the conditions as seen from an advocacy group's perspective, a memo to a legislator by an aide summarizing policy options. This guide holds the spotlight on such communications.

Who Is the Intended Audience?

Primarily, this book addresses undergraduate and graduate students of public policy, political science, public administration, public discourse, writing, and communication, along with their teachers.

Entry-level professionals in government, management, nonprofit organization, politics, public policy, public relations, public affairs, public administration, social work, or public health will find the guide useful.

Active citizens who are engaged in community issues, politics, or government, or those who serve in civic organizations, will find the guide useful, too.

For these audiences, *Writing Public Policy: A Practical Guide to Communicating in the Policy Making Process* teaches kinds of writing and speaking that are commonly practiced in the institutional process of solving public problems in a political democracy.

Special Features of This Book

You will find the following learning strategies here:

- Case illustrations and scenarios showing the policy making process in cultural context
- Writing samples by professionals, students, and citizens participating in government and nonprofit organizations
- Commentary to show how the writing samples apply communication principles, perform thinking or communication tasks, and meet expected standards
- A general method for communicating, with checklists for planning, producing, and assessing documents
- Specific instructions for selected document types

Every scenario and sample is taken from actual or simulated policy work. Most represent the work of professionals in government or nonprofit organizations; some represent the work of students in classroom simulations; a few represent both, as the student work produced in classroom simulation crossed over into use in a governmental process. The samples are just that, samples by real writers, not models.

They are work products, presented as written. (In some, omissions to reduce length and requested alterations are indicated.)

The cases, scenarios, and samples provide a realistic and multifaceted overview of the policy process and its written products without oversimplification. This guide's immersion approach to developing know-how assumes that broad exposure lets you develop feel for the territory and a sense of its predictability as well as variability. Consequently, this guide does not present a singular case of policy making to which all the scenarios and samples relate. Instead, you will find exemplification drawn from multiple policy processes. Coherence is provided by sustained topics (health and safety, for instance) that turn up in this guide like themes in a novel. Coherence also comes from the presence of exemplars, or communicators who turn up in several chapters to show a writer producing documents to progress through phases of a policy process.

Given the real demands of public policy making, this guide assumes that communicators in the process need both general know-how and specific skills. General know-how, or the ability to consider contexts and situations rhetorically, strategically, and ethically, is important. Ability to judge a communication's potential impact matters, too. Specific skills for composing expected, specific types of communication are obviously necessary. Consequently, to meet both needs, a general method of rhetorical and strategic planning is provided here, along with detailed task-by-task instructions for commonly used genres or types of communication. Together, the method and instructions provide a disciplined approach to writing and speaking successfully under typical working conditions of public policy activity.

Limits of this guide should be noted. First, the emphasis is on communicating in, or with, government. The emphasis is justifiable because government makes most public policy and because people know too little about what government does and does not do. Other actors are certainly involved. Here, they are included as influences on the process as it occurs in the governmental framework. For example, while it is true that large-scale corporate or religious or educational institutions indirectly make public policy by the effect of their independent actions, those actors are addressed here as influences on governmental policy making.

Second, less familiar types of institutional communication are included here while more familiar types of mass communication are excluded. Witness testimony in legislative hearings and public comment in administrative rule making are inclued because they are neglected in writing instruction. Press releases are excluded because instruction in their creation and use is widely available. Good advice on creating press kits is found in *The Insider's Guide to Political Internships* (185–94), for example.

Finally, some types of policy documentation cannot be adequately addressed in a compact guide. However, the guidance on writing in policy workplaces offered here is broadly applicable, both to the selected document types included here and beyond.

What is New in the Second Edition?

- Updated and new illustrations, scenarios, and samples to show persistent themes and emerging topics in current public policy making;
- A global perspective to show policy problems and communication practices in different national contexts;
- More professional samples to illustrate varied policy workplaces;
- Streamlined linkage of scenarios, samples, and commentary on the samples;
- Key concepts and further readings for each chapter;
- An appendix on writing for the Web in government, nongovernmental organizations, and civic activity;
- An appendix on clear writing;

Acknowledgments

This book results from my interaction with professionals and executives in federal and state government, elected and appointed officeholders in local government, and undergraduate and graduate policy writing students at three universities. Among them are Kathy Karlson of the U.S. Government Accountability Office (GAO) Training Institute and my GAO training co-leader, JoAnn Crandall, formerly of the Center for Applied Linguistics, who introduced me to government communication. The know-how and skill of executives and professionals at GAO (too many to list) set the book's aims. For permitting my use of their policy work experience and writing samples, I specially thank Syracuse University undergraduates Elizabeth Graves, Nicholas Alexander, Randy Ali, Sandra Derstine, Felicia Feinerman, Alaina Miller, Lisa Mueller, and Jennifer Salomon, as well as East Carolina University graduates Ashley O'Neill, Michael Cavanagh, Cliff Nelson, and Joseph Dawson. Similarly, for contribution of experience and samples, I thank (former) Orange County (North Carolina) Commissioner Margaret W. Brown, Gregg Township (Pennsylvania) supervisor Douglas P. Bierly, Penns Valley (Pennsylvania) Conservation Association board members, Pennsylvania Association for Sustainable Agriculture executive director Brian Snyder, and (former) Policy Director of the U.S. Department of Transportation's National Highway and Traffic Safety Administration Carl E. Nash.

Administrators, faculty colleagues, and community friends have provided materials, advice, or vital support for the book project. Syracuse University's College of Arts and Sciences supported an experimental undergraduate course in writing public policy from which the book's plan developed. East Carolina University's English Department and Continuing Studies, as well as the University of North Carolina-Chapel Hill's Public Policy Department and William and Ida Friday Center for Continuing Education, have brought new contributors to the book through distance education.

John B. Smith and Carl E. Nash encouraged and helped the project in countless ways. For contributions to individual chapters, I gratefully acknowledge Syracuse University's William D. Coplin, Carol Dwyer, and Frank Lazarski of the Public Affairs Program in the Maxwell School of Citizenship and Public Policy; Natasha Cooper and Lesley Pease of the E. S. Bird Library; and Stephen Thorley, Frederick Gale, and Molly Voorheis of the Writing Program. I also acknowledge the University of North Carolina-Chapel Hill's Krista Perreira, Daniel Gitterman, Mort Webster, Lucy S. Gorham, Jessica L. Dorrance, and Sudhanshu Handa of the Public Policy Department.

Special thanks to Jan Ehrler, political consultant and information designer at idheap (Institut de Hautes Études en Administration

Publique) in Switzerland for permitting use of his visualization of the policy cycle.

Special thanks to Stephen Thorley and Molly Voorheis of Syracuse University for critiquing the book from the government professional's and writing teacher's perspectives. Special thanks to Susan Warner-Mills, Jinx Crouch, and Suzanne D. LaLonde for critiquing it from the active citizen's perspective. Thanks to George Rhinehart, Heather Rosso, and Alex Bierly for expert manuscript preparation for the first edition. Special thanks to East Carolina University's Cliff Nelson and Daniel Siepert for skilled research assistance, editing, and manuscript preparation for the second edition.

The first edition benefited from manuscript reviews by Robert V. Bartlett, Purdue University; Charles Bazerman, University of California, Santa Barbara; Marie Danziger, Harvard University; Amy Devitt, University of Kansas; James Dubinsky, Virgina Tech; Daniel Gitterman, University of North Carolina, Chapel Hill; David Kaufer, Carnegie Mellon; Joe Olson, Pennsylvania State University; Carolyn Rude, Virginia Tech; and Susan Tolchin, George Mason University. The second edition benefited from manuscript reviews by teachers who had used the guide: R. Steven Daniels, California State University, Bakersfield; Brian Ellison, Appalachian State University; Roger Green, Florida Gulf Coast University; Jeff Gulati, Bentley College; John A. Hamman, Southern Illinois University; Maria Martinez-Cosio, University of Texas, Arlington; Greg McAvoy, University of North Carolina, Greensboro; Alice Philbin, James Madison University; David Pitts, Georgia State University; and Larry Rosenthal, University of California, Berkeley. I incorporated many of their thoughtful suggestions in revising. Oxford University Press Assistant Editor Cory Schneider expertly guided the second edition's production as did Executive Editor Jan Beatty and Production Editor Brian Black. Thanks also to former acquisitions editor Tony English, who first signed the project for the Press.

Reference

Reeher, G. and M. Mariani. 2002. *The insider's guide to political internships.* Boulder, CO: Westview Press.

Introduction:
How to Use This Book

To benefit from this book, you do not need prior experience as a student of public policy, as an intern in government, as a student in community-based learning, as an activist in campus or community affairs, or as a volunteer in a nonprofit organization. Any such experience will be very helpful, and you can draw on it often as you use this book. But it is not required. Experience or training in professional or business or administrative communication will be helpful, too, but it is not required.

You will find this book useful if

- you are majoring in the social sciences or humanities to prepare for a career in politics, government, public relations, law, public policy, journalism, social work, or public health;

- you are (or might in the future be) an intern in government, in a think tank, or in a nongovernmental organization concerned with public affairs;

- you are preparing to enter (or you are already practicing in) a publicly regulated industry or business;

- you have (or seek) a job as a communications aide in government or a political action organization;

- you have (or seek) a job as a public policy/public relations director in a nonprofit organization or as a public affairs liaison in a corporation, trade organization, professional association, or community service agency;

- you are a writer, and you write about public affairs;
- you are concerned about a local, national, or world problem, and you want to do something about it;
- you want or are asked to comment publicly on a controversy and you do not feel you have the authority or knowledge or skill to do that.

How Should You Use This Book?

It is a manual of practice, or guide, so you can use it whenever you have a wish or face a demand to enter a public forum or to participate in a public policy making process. Here's the intended model of use, whether you are a student, professional, or active citizen. You bring experience, knowledge, willingness to learn, persistence, and a motivating topic of concern. In the book, first read the foundational chapters 1 and 2. Before you write (or speak) on the topic of concern, answer general questions about the policy process (General Method, chapter 2) to make yourself aware of the cultural context and the rhetorical situation of your intended communication, and to plan the product. Then follow the specific instructions (chapters 3 through 9) to compose the product with awareness of the context and your plan. After you compose, use the checklists of expected qualities in policy communications (chapter 2) to assess the product. Revise it as necessary before communicating it.

Do you need all of the book or only parts? That depends on your intentions and circumstances. The chapters build on one another, but they can be used separately. If you are a student in a policy writing course, you might use this entire book. Start with a topic of concern; then compose the necessary communications to "work" the topic through a typical policy process. The benefits of using the entire book are that writers gain increased knowledge of a topic and an overview of the policy making process while developing competencies in an integrated set of communication practices. For a collaborative project, writers might divide up the communication responsibilities and designate individuals to produce particular documents or presentations using relevant chapters. That way, individuals gain practical experience with one or more of the types of communication while the group collectively gains an overview of the process.

If you are learning independently to meet a particular demand, use the chapters that fit the demand.

If you feel intimidated because you don't know enough about a subject or about policy making or about policy writing, do not worry. Your knowledge will grow as you practice the communications this book teaches. (This encouragement comes to you directly from evaluations by students who used this book.)

Before getting underway, read chapters 1 (on public policy) and 2 (on communicating in the culture of policy work). If you are starting with only a concern, you will know much more about the topic after you conduct the necessary inquiry (as an advocate) or analysis (as a policy analyst) to define the topic as a public policy problem (chapter 3). You will learn how to relate your definition of the problem to other definitions, interests, and viewpoints by answering questions intended to prompt your awareness of the cultural context of policy making (chapter 2).

You will learn about the institutional process by searching public records for prior government action on the problem (chapter 4).

At that point, you may feel overwhelmed by the amount of available information on your topic of concern. However, with confidence gained in prior learning, you will start to filter for relevant information as you clarify your position and plan your argument on solving the problem (chapter 5).

Informed about existing (or absent) policy on the topic, you can identify a need for policy, a beneficial reform, or a better alternative (chapter 6). When opportunity comes or obligation demands, you'll be ready to communicate your advocacy or analysis in a public forum or policy process (chapters 7, 8, and 9).

Tip: Several chapters (3, 4, and 8) anticipate research and communication tasks that may be given without much warning to interns, volunteers, and professionals new on the job, ready or not. If that happens to you, after first reviewing chapter 2 on communicating in context, you might find chapter 3 on problem definition, chapter 4 on legislative records research, and chapter 8 on witness testimony particularly helpful.

While reading, pay attention to the features of this book that are intended to help you learn. Overall, this text provides a general method for communicating and includes checklists for planning, producing, and assessing documents. To illustrate applications of this method, writing samples by professionals, students, and citizens participating in government and nonprofit organizations are presented throughout the book. These samples are accompanied by commentary that shows how they apply communication principles, perform thinking or communication tasks, and meet expected standards. In addition, case illustrations and scenarios show the policy making process in cultural context. Finally, specific instructions for selected document types are provided.

List of Writing Samples

CHAPTER 1

Public Policy Making

Key Concepts

- Problem solving process
- Governmental framework
- Pluralism

This guide to communication is informed by the idea of public policy making as a democratic process of solving problems. This chapter frames the process from the perspective of communication and offers two illustrative cases. Other ways to think about public policy making are found in suggested readings at the end of this chapter.

Public policy exists to solve problems affecting people in society (Coplin and O'Leary 1998). Making public policy means deciding what is and is not a problem, choosing which problems to solve, and deciding on solutions. The process occurs in a political context of pluralism. Problems are conceived and defined differently by variously interested actors. Solutions are achieved through mutual adjustment and adaptation of interests. Decision often demands compromise and reflects institutional constraints. The framework for decision is governmental.

Case 1: Milk Labeling

On October 24, 2007, Pennsylvania announced a new standard of food safety aimed to prevent "mislabeling" of food products, especially "misleading" labels. That's *public policy*, a standing decision by government. An administrative agency, the state's department of agriculture, targeted dairy food as the problem. Specifically, milk produced or sold in Pennsylvania could not be labeled as "hormone-free." Labels could not say that milk came from cows not treated with "artificial growth hormone" or with "rBGH" or "rBST," common acronyms for recombinant bovine somatotropine growth hormone.

Politics influenced the decision. Arguably, the agency's decision to target milk labeling favored one set of stakeholders, the maker of rBST and dairy farmers who use it. That coalition had long argued that milk labels saying "no artificial growth hormone" or similar language harmed sales of their products by implying that milk from cows treated with rBST is unsafe. They cited Federal Drug Administration approval for rBST use and scientific evidence of its safety. The state agriculture secretary agreed.

The agency's decision was immediately controversial in Pennsylvania and elsewhere. News and reaction spread through newspaper, telephone, email, blogs, and chat outlets. Dairy farmers who did not use rBST and who wanted to say they did not on milk labels organized rapidly to oppose the ban. Advocates for sustainable agriculture joined these farmers in coalition. They counterargued that the science on rBST's safety is inconclusive, that farmers have a right to inform consumers about their product, and that consumers have the right to make informed choices. Plans for litigation against the state were announced. In parallel action, farmers who did use rBST organized to react in coalition with other advocacy groups in support of the ban.

In mid-November, Pennsylvania's governor postponed the ban, and then cancelled it. On January 17, 2008, the governor along with the secretary of agriculture announced two policy changes, a revised standard for dairy product labeling and new procedures for oversight of labeling claims. Under rule revisions, labels are permitted to claim that milk came from cows not treated with rBST along with a disclaimer as to its potential for health risk. Dairy food processors are required to verify label claims by having dairy farmers sign affidavits regarding production methods. That's *policy making* in institutional democracy.

This snapshot captures the basics. For a more complete view of this case, read participants' own communications. They reveal dimensions of debate, and they illustrate a typical mix of policy writing styles. Extracts selected from key participants' statements are presented below. To read the full text of these and related communications, go to the source cited. The following extracts start with the state's initial announcement and follow the story as it developed.

Government Chooses a Problem

Memorandum
To: Agriculture and Food Labeling Stakeholders
From: Secretary Dennis C. Wolff
Subject: Product Label Review Update
Date: October 23, 2007

The Pennsylvania Department of Agriculture (PDA) is increasingly being made aware of concerns from consumers, farmers, and public policy makers regarding mislabeled food products. These include concerns as to whether label claims are accurate and verifiable, and whether label claims are misleading.

For example, concerns have been raised that some labels are misleading consumers by promoting what is *not* in the product...I recently called upon help from a group of dietitians, consumer advocates, and food industry representatives on current issues relating to food labeling by establishing the Food Labeling Advisory Committee...While widespread food labeling concerns existed, the Committee recommendation is to begin by addressing dairy labeling improprieties. This is a logical starting point, in that PDA has current legal responsibility to review certain milk and dairy product labels before they are used in commerce.

Local and National Media Disseminate the News and Opinion

"Milk-Labeling and Marketing Integrity"
By Hon. Dennis C. Wolff, Pennsylvania Secretary of Agriculture, *Lancaster Farming,* November 3, 2007.

Consumers rely upon the labeling of a product when deciding what to buy for their families. Recently, concern has risen over the way milk products are labeled and the Department of Agriculture has taken action to help consumers make informed decisions about what to buy and to feed their families.

Some labels mislead by promoting what is not in the product, a practice called absence labeling. This marketing strategy is confusing and implies a safe versus not safe product.

[Additional content omitted.]

I take issue with the fact that companies use false food labeling tactics to gain a market advantage…Ultimately, we are seeking a solution to the labeling issue that will benefit those who produce Pennsylvania's food and those who consume it.

"Consumers Won't Know What They're Missing"

By Andrew Martin, NYTimes.com, The Feed, November 11, 2007. http://www.nytimes.com/2007/11/11/business/11feed.html?_r=2&oref=slogin&oref=slogin

The Pennsylvania Department of Agriculture has decided that consumers are too dim to make their own shopping decisions. Agriculture officials in Ohio are contemplating a similar decision….

Dairy Farmers React to Oppose the Ban

Opinion by Todd Rutter, dairy farmer, president of Rutter's Dairy in York, Pennsylvania. *Harrisburg Patriot News*, November 9, 2007. Quoted in Sherry Bunting, "Milk Label Issue Comes to a Boil in Pennsylvania," *Farmshine*, November 16, 2007; reprinted in Consumer Attitudes About Biotechnology, Science & Education, rbST Public Discussion, Penn State Dairy and Animal Science Blogs, Terry Etherton Blog on Biotechnology. http://blogs.das.psu.edu/tetherton/2007/11/17/milk-label-issue-comes-to-a-boil-in-pennsylvania/

…The state's untenable position has only emboldened Rutter's in this regard, prompting us to plan a series of very public activities designed to educate the community and our customers about artificial growth hormones and our strong stance against their use in our milk production, not to mention our right to say so on our labels.

In the next couple of weeks, we will be running full-page newspaper ads, handing out more than 100,000 information cards through Rutter's Farm Stores, posting content at http://www.rutters.com, and, on Nov. 13, hand-delivering letters to every member of the Pennsylvania General Assembly. Of course, we're also pursuing all legal avenues available to us to protect our right to provide consumer information.

Dairy Farmers React to Support the Ban

Opinion by Daniel Brandt, dairy farmer, Annville, Pennsylvania; PA Holstein Association State Director; Lebanon County Farm Bureau Director, November 17, 2007 at 12:16 pm. Filed under Consumer Attitudes About Biotechnology, Science & Education, rbST Public Discussion, Penn State Dairy and Animal Science Blogs, Terry Etherton Blog on Biotechnology. http://blogs.das.psu.edu/tetherton/2007/11/17/rutter-hormone-stutter/

In Todd Rutter's little rant in the November 9th *Harrisburg Patriot News*, it is shameful that he had no scientific documents to back up his claims...He does nothing to promote milk for what it is and the unprecedented benefits of drinking milk....

Advocates Opposing the Ban Reframe the Debate

"Time to Do the Right Thing with Food Labeling"
Email action alert, November 11, 2007 by Brian Snyder, Executive Director, Pennsylvania Association for Sustainable Agriculture, http://pasafarming.org; Leslie Zuck, Executive Director, Pennsylvania Certified Organic, http://www.paorganic.org; Timothy LaSalle, CEO, The Rodale Institute, http://www.rodaleinstitute.org

On its face, the recent decision by the Pennsylvania Department of Agriculture to conduct a crackdown on what it considers to be false or misleading claims on dairy product labels may seem to be in everyone's best interest....The essential question to ask is "What's really in everyone's best interest over the long term?"...The whole labeling controversy itself is only a sideshow to the real issues involved here, which have more to do with ethics and the industry-perceived need for the use of performance enhancing drugs in livestock production...The use of artificial growth hormones (rBST or rBGH) is certainly not the only example of such drugs being used on farms today. In fact, the majority of antibiotics sold in America are actually used in livestock production as growth promoting agents, not as treatment for disease in humans or animals as many uninformed, potentially confused consumers might assume.

   ...By all means, it makes perfect sense to employ the "precautionary principle" when research on any aspect of food production is not conclusive—in doing so, the countries of Canada, Australia, New Zealand, Japan and all 25 members of the European Union have already banned the use of rBST/rBHG in the production of milk.

   So what's so wrong if an individual farmer or group of them working together wishes to advertise, even on a label, the choice made not to use such drugs at all, or at least not unless clinically indicated? While we are so busy debating when and how it is proper to put an absence claim on food labels, when do we get to consider the value of being completely forthcoming with consumers and letting them make informed choices?

Expert Comments

"rBST Certified Milk: A Story of Smoke and Mirrors"
By Terry Etherton, Distinguished Professor of Animal Nutrition and Head of the Department of Dairy and Animal Science, The Pennsylvania State University, October 3, 2006 at 4:23 pm. Filed under Agricultural Biotechnology, The Food System, rbST Public Discussion Penn State Dairy and Animal Science Blogs, Terry Etherton Blog on Biotechnology. http://blogs.das.psu.edu/tetherton/2006/10/03/rbst-certified-free-milk-a-story-of-smoke-and-mirrors/

The *Boston Globe* ran a story on Sept. 25th on the decision by H.P. Hood and Dean Foods to switch New England milk processing plants to "rbST-free" milk. In this story, a spokesperson for Dean Foods said, "Even though conventional milk is completely safe and...recombinant bovine somatotropin (rbST) is completely safe, some people don't feel comfortable with it"...There's little doubt that consumers who have no understanding are easily gulled by such labels..."If the future of our industry is based on marketing tactics that try to sway consumers with 'good milk' versus 'bad milk' messages, we are all in trouble," Kevin Holloway, President of Monsanto Dairy, told a group of dairy producers at a September 13th meeting in Washington D.C....

   The reality I have observed is that it is easy to scare the public in a 30-second media message. It is impossible to give them a sound scientific understanding about the benefits of biotechnology in the barnyard in 30 seconds...One can ask, who wins? Junk science by a knockout....

Government Revises the Policy

"Governor Rendell says Consumers Can Have Greater Confidence in Milk Labels"

Office of the Governor, Commonwealth of Pennsylvania, Press Release, November 17, 2007.

Governor Edward G. Rendell today announced that labels informing customers the milk they intend to buy is produced without rBST...can continue to be used...under new guidelines for accountability. "The public has a right to complete information about how the milk they buy is produced," said Governor Rendell.

Government Promulgates a New Ruling

William Chirdon, Bureau Director, Commonwealth of Pennsylvania, Department of Agriculture, Bureau of Food Safety and Laboratory Services.

Dear Fluid Milk Permit Holder...PDA has received a great deal of input on the standards set forth [in October 2007]...Enclosed please find a new document titled 'Revised Standards and Procedure for the Approval of Proposed Labeling of Fluid Milk' dated January 17, 2008...Please review this document carefully and govern yourself accordingly....

From the revised standard:

"7. Label Representations.

(A) No labeling may be false or misleading....

    i. In no instance shall any label state or imply that milk from cows not treated with recombinant bovine somatotropin (rBST, rbST, RBST, or rbst) differs in composition from milk products made with milk from treated cows....

    ii. No labeling may contain references such as 'No Hormones, Hormone Free,....

    [Additional content omitted.]

(B) Permitted Claims. The following claims are permitted:
   (i) RBST (referenced to FDA February 10, 1994 Guidance on the Voluntary Labeling of Milk....)
   1. 'From cows not treated with rBST. No significant difference has been found between milk derived from rBST-treated and non-rBST treated cows' or a substantial equivalent. Hereinafter, the first sentence shall be referred to as the 'Claim' and the second sentence shall be referred to as the 'Disclaimer....'

...(Standards   2.0.1.17.08.   http://www.agriculture.state.pa.us/ agriculture/lib/agriculture/foodsafetyfiles/labeling/milk_labeling_ standards_new.pdf)

Advocates Opposing the Ban Reflect on the Outcome

"A Day for Celebration and Humility"

By Brian Snyder, Pennsylvania Association for Sustainable Agriculture. Email, January 1, 2008.

This is truly a cause for celebration for all of us, especially those who responded to our alerts by sending letters and emails or making phone calls to Governor Rendell's office and the Pennsylvania Department of Agriculture....This is also a day for reflection and humility. There were many farmers on both sides of this issue right from the start, and the damage done to the agricultural community in Pennsylvania will take some time to heal...Yesterday's announcement preserved the right of farmers to communicate with eaters about the way food is being produced in a straightforward way. If you think about it, this is just about as fundamental as it gets.

News Media Reports Ongoing Advocacy Supporting the Ban

"Fighting on a Battlefield the Size of a Postage Stamp"

By Andrew Martin, The Feed, nytimes.com, March 9, 2009. http://www.nytimes.com/2008/03/09/business/09feed.html

A new advocacy group closely tied to Monsanto has started a counteroffensive to stop the proliferation of milk that comes from cows that aren't treated with synthetic bovine growth hormone. The group, called American Farmers for the Advancement and Conservation of Technology, or Afact, says it is a grass-roots organization that came together to defend members' right to use recombinant bovine somatotropin, also known as rBST or rBGH....

National News Media Reports Continuing Debate

"'Hormone-free' milk spurs labeling debate"
Christian Science Monitor, April 21, 2008. http://www.csmonitor.com/2008/0421/p13s01-sten.html?page=1April

Ohio, Missouri, Kansas, Indiana, and Michigan all have pending legislation or rule changes that would limit labeling claims about hormones...Some say Monsanto is behind attempts to remove mentions of hormones. "Clearly what's going on is Monsanto is trying to get states to thwart the market from working," says Michael Hansen, senior scientist for Consumers Union...But Monsanto contends that milk from cows treated with [its rBST product called] Posilac is safe...Monsanto has unsuccessfully petitioned the Federal Trade Commission for a rule change about what it says is deceptive labeling. Other legal action taken by the company and lobbying by farm bureaus to block such labeling has largely failed. Legal precedent appears to uphold the free-speech interest of dairies and the consumer's right to know...As other new agricultural technology reaches the market, labeling debates appear likely to increase, industry analysts say. For example, milk made from cloned animals and their offspring, approved January 15, 2008 by the FDA, has already prompted one labeling bill in California..."This [milk labeling] issue will not go away, says the Consumer Union's Mr. Hansen."

What this case shows. Common features of policy making are illustrated here. For example, this case shows typical complexity in defining the problem. At least five policy problems with associated issues are conceivable in this case: (1) agricultural biotechnology with issues of impacts on people, animals, and ecosystems; (2) food safety with issues of consumer protection; (3) labeling with issues of free speech; (4) trade with issues of marketing and advertising; (5) ethics with issues of conflicting values. These conceptions of the problem are not mutually exclusive. That's typical, too. Problems usually are blends.

Solutions are selective. Policy analysis considers the options. In this case, basic options were considered. The state could accept the status quo without further action, or it could intervene, perhaps with limitations. To accept the status quo, Pennsylvania could follow federal Food and Drug Administration guidelines that allow rBST use in milk production and do not call for labeling. Instead, the state chose to regulate labeling, first to ban a specific practice, then later to allow it with limitations.

In the governmental framework, all three branches, the legislature, executive and administration, and judiciary make public policy. This case illustrates administrative policy making that involves federal and state government. The federal agency acted to the limit of its authority to monitor food safety, where the state agency went on to act within its authority to monitor product labeling.

Debate about the use of scientific evidence in policy making emerged in this case. On the subject of rBST use, United States, Canadian, and European Union policies differ, with the United States permitting the use and the other governments not permitting it. The variation is attributable partly to different interpretations of evidence and partly to international differences in regulatory agencies' power.

Communication technology's impact on public process is evident in this case. Far exceeding print media's impact on opinion in rural communities, the Internet's capacity to rapidly distribute information by email, online news, blogs, chat, and other media altered and accelerated Pennsylvania's process. Elsewhere, in other states, the network of information helped to organize interest groups across boundaries as more state governments took up the problem. Continuing access to online news archives kept the unofficial public record open and the issues alive as the problem moved beyond Pennsylvania.

Policy making is not always as topical or as visible as in the milk-labeling case. Important policy work goes quietly on every day in governance. Budgeting is a good example. Communications move a budget cycle along. To illustrate, an actual state budget development is described next, shown from the viewpoint of the communications director for the state senate's budget committee chairman.

Case 2: Budgeting

The annual state budgeting process occurs over 6 months with preset deadlines or milestones. In January, the governor proposes a budget for the coming year that represents the administration's priorities and politics. The legislative committees respond in March (for the house) and in May (for the senate) with recommendations based on their priorities and politics. Effectively, three budget proposals—the governor's, the house's, and the senate's—must culminate in a single adopted budget by July 1, the mandated start of the state's new fiscal year.

In early January, a state governor holds a press conference to announce the release of his proposed budget for the coming year. Immediately after the governor's press conference, the chairs of the state's house of representatives and senate budget committees comment publicly on the governor's proposed budget in other press conferences, newspaper interviews, and radio and television talk show appearances. The communications director for the senate budget chair tracks public response to the governor's budget and to the senate chair's comments on it.

At the same time, work begins on the senate and house budget recommendations. In the senate, the current chair of the ways and means committee brings his staff (an administrative assistant and the communications director) to a meeting with staff for the permanent committee. Present are the ways and means chief of staff, chief legal counsel, and chief budget analyst. The chair has authority, as a member of the majority political party, to set the senate's current budget policy. The permanent committee staff has responsibility for developing, with the help of the chair's staff, the senate's recommendations for budgeting according to current priorities.

In the first meeting in January, the chair and the combined staffs review budget history (what's carried over from last year and what's new this year), the state of the economy (current and projected conditions), and the politics of individual budget items (item is nice to have but can be sacrificed if necessary, item is nonnegotiable, we expect a fight on the item, or we go to the mat with the item). They compile a rough list of potential priorities for the coming year's budget. Because he will draft text for the senate recommendations, the communications director starts taking notes.

After the first meeting, the committee staff fans out in January and February to consult with federal and state fiscal experts, as well as with experts on specific issues in state agencies, government watchdog groups, and advocacy groups. They get more projections for the economy, and they seek external corroboration for their rough list of budget priorities. The communications director goes along to all these consultations.

Next, the committee staff solicits budget requests internally from senate members, state departments, and state agencies. Staffers meet with the members, departments, and agencies about their requests. They begin an initial breakdown of line items to include in the senate recommendations. The communications director stays in touch with the staff. In parallel, he maintains daily or weekly contact with editors and reporters of major news media. He develops relationships and educates the press. They, in turn, keep him up-to-date on budget-relevant news. He maintains good contact both internally and externally because he has dual responsibilities to anticipate debate about the senate's recommendations and to present them in a way that will promote their acceptance by government officials and the public.

A second working meeting is held. The chair and combined staffs intensely debate priorities and preliminarily decide on key priorities. Later in March, when the house budget proposal is released, the combined staffs analyze it, compare it with the governor's proposal, and compare it with their own developing proposal. The communications director participates in the meetings and continues to track press and public responses to the governor's proposal and to the house recommendations. Most important, he translates the key priorities (decided at the second working meeting) into key messages, simple statements that identify a key issue, and the senate's proposed way of using tax dollars to address the issue. He gets the chair's and committee senior staff's commitment to emphasize the key messages at every communication opportunity. Whenever they speak or write, they agree that the key messages will be appropriately included.

Throughout March and April, the senate budget committee staff finalizes its recommendations and interacts with the governor's and house committee's staffs. The communications director's attention increasingly turns to his primary responsibility of drafting the document that will both present senate recommendations and publicize them; he must also prepare for debate in the legislature and for negotiation with the governor's office during the budget approval process.

In March, he writes preliminary drafts of the chairman's introduction and the executive summary for the document. (He knows that when the lengthy and detailed document is released, many people, including the press, will read only the chair's introduction and the executive summary.) He emphasizes the key messages in both. He writes (or edits senior staff's) descriptions of major budget categories (health care, education, housing, and so forth). From his notes taken in budget working meetings, he develops arguments to support proposed dollar figures for existing line items and new initiatives in each category.

Also in March, he plans a comprehensive internal and external presentation strategy to be carried out in June. Along with internal distribution to the governor, the legislature, and government departments and agencies, the senate's recommendations will be publicized through an external news media and public events campaign conducted before, during, and after formal release of the recommendations document.

In April and early May, he revises the document based on committee staffers' review of his preliminary drafts and edits of their drafts. He coordinates with news media and advocacy groups regarding a public relations campaign to accompany release of the senate recommendations. By mid-May, the finished 600-page document presenting the recommendations is delivered to the printer. He fields inquiries by the press and the public about the soon-to-be-released recommendations, and he focuses on writing, editing, and revising press releases; other public announcements; and the chairman's comments for the senate budget release press conference.

In late May, the senate recommendations are released, distributed, and announced. Simultaneously, the planned public relations campaign is conducted. Throughout June, while the senate and house debate the budget and the governor responds to their debates, events all around the state (preplanned jointly by the communications director and advocacy groups) direct public attention to senate priorities and funding proposals during "health care week" or "education week" or "citizenship assistance week." Meanwhile, back in the senate, the communications director puts out daily press releases, follows up phone contacts by the press or the public, and prepares comments for the chair's use in responding to unexpected developments, politically significant news, or budget controversies.

What this case shows. The problem here is the need to finance state government operations and public services in the coming year. The problem solving process is the annual budgeting cycle. The major actors are three elected officials (the governor and the chairs of the state senate and house of representatives budget committees). Five appointed professional staffs (the governor's, the two chairs', and the two committees') advise and assist the elected officials. Other players are experts inside and outside state government with knowledge on specific topics, policy analysts who will advise authorities on ways to approach the problem, and advocates representing special civic, commercial, or political interests in the solution. The resulting policy is a set of priorities and related recommendations for spending.

In this case, you might be able to see components of policy making functioning in a flow of actions to conduct a process. In budgeting, basic institutional actions are to define priorities in relation to current conditions and goals; to review previous goals; to take reasoned positions on needs, argue for them, and negotiate with others who reason differently; to propose specific objectives and spending levels; to deliberate alternative proposals and decide; and to inform and invite public participation. The flow of activity in this particular process is typical of institutional policy making.

Typical integration of communication and action is shown here, too. Communication products formalize conceptions and enable further action. For example, what most people call "the budget" is not the policy itself but rather an intentionally persuasive document (composed by the communications director, in this instance) that argues for objectives based on the priorities and that proposes funding allocations to accomplish them. It is the last of many documents that move the process along. At earlier stages, working discussions are materialized in draft documents. Circulation of the drafts for comment, editing, and revision facilitates negotiation about priorities. With persuasive expression and specific figures, the final budget document serves both general public discourse (persuasive expression of priorities and objectives) and institutional discourse (specific figures) about governmental spending in the coming year.

Practical communications in this case deserve comment, too. From a communicator's viewpoint, budgeting, while orderly as a policy cycle, is quite messy as a real process. The case illustrates the typical density of information, number of writing demands, need to balance competing interests, need to coordinate actors, even the juggling of schedules that characterize a policy process and create the working conditions for communicators.

Detailed exemplification such as the milk labeling and budgeting cases gives you a material, real-time view of the policy process. Visualization gives you an abstract view. The graphic in Figure 1.1 organizes the phases of policy making into a progression of discrete and different actions.

In Figure 1.1, the initial phases of generating public interest and selecting a problem progress to designing a political solution or policy and deciding on a course of action to carry out its intent. Decision then progresses to implementation and administration labeled in the graphic as output, impact, and outcome. Implementation continues through evaluation, which leads to decision either to improve and continue the policy or to terminate it. Essential communications at each phase of the cycle are not shown. Instead, a separate category, documentation, appears early in this abstract view as an indicator.

Like the list of policy actions in the preface to this book, Figure 1.1 simplifies reality. This cyclic view portrays policy making as progressing (lines and arrows) predictably through distinct phases (boxes). While it's too linear, a cyclic view nonetheless is helpful, if only because it encourages optimism. When you are immersed in grinding details or frustrating politics of policy work and it feels as if you are getting nowhere, it's refreshing to remember that you are engaging a process, however messy, with short-term objectives and long-term goals.

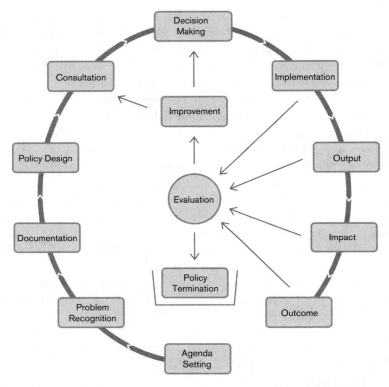

Figure 1.1 The public policy cycle (By permission of Jan Ehrler, inffab, Switzerland).

Summary and Preview

Public policy making has three basic components: the problem, the policy, and the process. A problem is a perceived wrong in society or its environment. A policy is a standing decision by government. The process is problem solving in pluralistic politics and a governmental framework.

Next, chapter 2 explains how communication functions in the process and offers a disciplined approach to policy writing and speaking.

Reference

Coplin, W. D., and M. K. O'Leary. 1998. *Public policy skills.* 3rd ed. Washington DC: Policy Studies Associates.

Further Reading

Baumgartner, F. R., and B. D. Jones. 1993. *Agendas and instability in American polit*ics. Chicago: University of Chicago Press.

Baumgartner, F. R., and B. D. Jones. 2002. *Policy dynamics.* Chicago: The University of Chicago Press.

Kingdon, J. W. 2003. *Agendas, alternatives, and public policies.* 2nd ed. New York: Longman.

Sabatier, P., ed. 1999. *Theories of the policy process.* Boulder, CO: Westview Press.

Stone, D. 2002. *Policy paradox: The art of political decision making.* rev. ed. New York: WW Norton.

CHAPTER 2

Communication in the Process

Key Concepts

- Communicating in the context of public policy making
- Communicating usefully
- Planning and producing communications

Writing and speaking are not sufficient to make public policy, but they are necessary.

Communication functions in two fundamental ways:

1. <u>Communication produces useful information</u>. Useful information in a public policy process has four major characteristics: it helps to solve problems, it serves action, it has consequences, and it is publicly accessible.

(i) Helps to solve problems: Every phase of a policy process—to frame a problem, to analyze issues, to argue approaches, to decide on solutions—demands information. <u>Only relevant information helps, however.</u> In deciding whether to provide information, always ask and answer these questions: To whom is this relevant? How will it help to solve the problem?

(ii) Serves action: In policy work, information makes things happen. In deciding whether and how to inform in a policy process, always ask and answer this question: What do I want this information to do?

(iii) Has consequences: A problem and its solution affect other problems and solutions in many contexts. Consequently, information's effects can be wide-ranging. In deciding whether and how to inform in a policy process, always ask and answer these questions: What is likely to happen as a result of this information? What impacts might this information have?

(iv) Is publicly accessible: Policy makers are answerable to the people who give them authority. Therefore, information used in public processes must be publicly available. Officially, it is recorded and preserved by government as an authoritative public record. Unofficially, news media of all kinds and people in everyday social interactions distribute information as well. In deciding whether and how to inform a policy process, always ask and answer this question: How will this information be made public?

2. Communication makes information intelligible in context. Context here means, narrowly, action in a particular policy cycle, or, broadly, a governmental framework and its political environment. Intelligibility means understanding achieved through activated knowledge of expectations. Presenters and recipients of information must have similar expectations, which a document (or talk) must activate in order for communication to occur.

What expectations? The most basic is genre knowledge, or the ability to recognize what type of communication is underway or is appropriate for the purpose. In policy work, genre knowledge grows as you understand the policy making process, the purposes associated with phases of a policy cycle, and the range of document or speech types conventionally used to create information for particular purposes. Experience in public policy work may be the best teacher, but you can also learn from others. This guide incorporates lessons learned by a range of policy communicators in order to develop your genre knowledge.

Another basic expectation is usefulness. In public policy communication, information is expected to be useful. What matters most is not how much you know but rather how much your readers or listeners know after they have read your document or heard your talk.

Finally, information is expected to be clearly, concisely, correctly, and credibly presented. Public policy work is information-overloaded. Especially in government and nonprofit organization settings, time is scarce, schedules are nearly impossible, and attention is always divided. Rarely does anybody have patience for disorganized, wordy documents that do not have an obvious purpose. Information functions best when it can be comprehended quickly, trusted as accurate, traced to authoritative sources, and used with confidence.

Cultural Context: Actors, Roles, and Communication Practices

Who generates public policy information? Actors in the policy making process do. Actors are participants. Actors create and use information in accord with their role in the process. As the term is used here, a role is a function or job with specific responsibility in the process.

Interests motivate actors and influence their role performance. Interests are stakes or concerns, which might be organized (collectively held, ready for action) or unorganized (individually held, latent). For example, a trade association or an advocacy group has organized interest, whereas a dispersed affected population has unorganized interest. Typically, organized interests acting as groups are most influential. However, individuals acting alone can be influential too.

For all actors, roles and interests might relate in complex ways, and lines between them can be unclear. Some ambiguity is normal, as when an elected officeholder represents constituency interests in seeking a particular committee assignment or in proposing legislation. But other ambiguity might be unethical, as when an officeholder communicates false information. Ethics guidelines and enforcement procedures, internal and external to government, protect the policy making process. Even better protection comes from consciously ethical actors who aim to do no harm.

Typical actors in public policy processes include the following:

- Providers of goods, services, or activities related to the problem
- Consumers of goods or services in the problem area (if organized)
- Experts with specialized knowledge of the problem
- Advocates and lobbyists representing particular interests in the problem
- Officials with authority to solve the problem

For example, in making policy for highway safety, the following actors would be involved:

- Automotive and insurance industries as providers of goods, services, or activities
- Organizations of automobile drivers as consumers
- Specialists in automobile design or analysts of the economics of transportation as experts
- Advocates for accident victims and lobbyists for law-enforcement associations as representatives of particular interests
- Members of Congress, cabinet secretaries, or state governors as official authorities

Whether they write or speak themselves or they authorize others to do it for them, policy actors generate information in relation to their role. Credibility, or the perceived reliability of information, is judged partly on the information source's role in the process. In the auto safety example, automotive industries credibly generate technical information on safety features of vehicles. Similarly, insurance industries credibly generate information on the economic consequences of accidents. Consumer groups credibly provide accounts of experience in using automotive products and credibly identify problematic conditions. Expert specialists in automobile design or materials credibly report results of research on ways to make cars safer. Expert policy analysts might credibly offer advice on policy options, such as regulation of manufacturers versus education of consumers. Advocates and lobbyists might credibly provide germane information about interested or affected groups, propose policy, and argue for or against policy based on group interests. Elected and appointed officials credibly generate the policy instruments, for instance, to reallocate funds, create a new program, or provide more oversight for existing programs.

Practical communications utilize forms conventionally expected to achieve a role's functions and particular purposes. Recall the typical actor roles in a policy process presented earlier in this chapter. For some of them, note the following examples of role-related practical communications. Elected and appointed legislative officials use bills and resolutions. Administrative officials use executive orders, statutes, legal codifications, standards and rules of enforcement, manuals, and press releases. (You can learn more about legislative and administrative communications in chapter 4 on government records research, where you are referred to respected sources, such as the Library of Congress's database Thomas that includes glossaries of government document types.) Advocates use position papers, research reports, action alerts, press releases, and witness testimony.

To suggest the range of practical policy communications, a listing that sorts actors by role and associated communication practices is provided next.

Professionals Inside Government

Within government, career or consulting professionals generate most of the working information of a policy process. They communicate in roles as, for example, legislative aides to members of a legislature, experts on the staffs of legislative committees, legal counsels to legislative committees and agencies, executive agency administrators, policy analysts, and technical specialists attached to many offices. To carry out their responsibilities, they might use any of the following document types:

- One-pagers (summaries of fact or perspective, limited to one page)
- Memos (more developed summaries of varying length)
- White papers (extensive reportage or analysis including evidence)
- Legislative concept proposals (outlines of model or idea or strategy for policy, without details)
- Legislative histories (reports of government action or inaction, based on government records)
- Committee reports (synthesis of committee decision and history of action on a topic)
- Speeches (to be delivered by elected or appointed officials)
- Testimonies (to be delivered by executives or professionals)

For some inside professionals, communication is the entire job. The communications director in the state budgeting case (chapter 1) is an example. A communications director is a generalist who

- writes and produces internal documents of many kinds;
- writes external public announcements of many kinds;
- produces kits of information for news media use.

Other professional communicators in government are specialists. They include

- speechwriters who draft talks for officials to deliver;
- legislation writers who draft bills for deliberation and formulate laws for codification;
- debate reporters who produce stenographic transcripts and the published records of deliberation and debate;
- webmasters who maintain government websites.

Professionals Outside Government

Significant amounts of information used in policy making come from outside government. Experts of many kinds in universities, industries, policy institutes, nonprofit organizations, and businesses write or contribute to white papers, reports of many kinds, and testimonies. Because they are not constrained as government employees are from engaging public debate, they may write opinion in print or online publications. The expert's blog in the milk labeling regulation example in chapter 1 exemplifies this practice. In addition, professionals and managers in publicly regulated industries and businesses might provide needed information.

For some outside professionals, communication for public policy purposes is the main focus of their job. Lobbyists are an example. They are experts in a subject and are employed by organizations to ensure that policy makers have information about the subject that is germane to the interests of the employing organizations and to ensure that policy makers are exposed to the full range of arguments on a given issue. Lobbyists might brief legislators and their staffs, or they might draft legislation for consideration. Policy analysts are a different example. They may be either inside or outside government. They are experts in using quantitative and qualitative methods to examine problems and options for solving problems. Analysts might advise policy makers on the choice of policy instruments or provide research results to aid the formulation of policy.

Active Citizens

Ordinary people in daily life inform and influence public policy making when they

- write or email officials;
- provide formal written remarks on their experience relevant to a problem or a policy in response to a call for comment;
- testify about effects of a problem or a policy on their life or their livelihood;
- conduct letter-writing campaigns, create email lists, and use phone trees;
- form a coalition to cooperate in solving a problem;
- create a mechanism, such as a lawsuit or a boycott, to force response by institutional authorities;
- lobby as a representative of civic organizations, trade associations, professional associations, communities of interest, or constituencies.

The milk labeling case in chapter 1 illustrates citizen participation in several of these ways.

A General Method of Communicating in a Public Process

In this chapter so far, you have been introduced to expectations and roles with associated communication practices typically found in public policy work.

Change reading gears here, please. What follows is a method for writing (or speaking) fitted to the culture of public policy making. It translates the culture into practical, routine questions you should ask when considering the motivation, context, and situation for a communication. At the end of the questions are two checklists that compile the expected qualities that public policy documents or talks should have. The checklists are intended for your use in assessing a policy document you have written or a talk you have planned.

Now, you should only read the outline and checklists for perspective and for familiarity. Later, when you have an actual need to communicate (for instance, in a course or a policy workplace), use the method to plan before you write. Use the checklists after you write.

If your writing experience has been mainly in the classroom, you may be surprised by the method's questions. They represent real world writing conditions. For quick orientation to real world writing, see any basic guide for professional communicators.

Ask and answer the method's questions to plan and produce a communication. They prompt you to consider all the usual components of a writing situation and to take note of significant particulars that might affect your work. Your answers to the questions are your guide to writing or planning the needed product.

Practice this procedure methodically (even if laboriously at first) until it becomes routine to ask these questions each time you have a need to communicate. At first, jotting down your answers and keeping your notes nearby as you write will be helpful. Later, when you habitually use this method to prepare for communicating, you will routinely adapt it to particular demands. A word of caution: Even if you skip some questions, do not omit whole steps in the method. All the steps are needed to cover the basics. Omitting a step in the preparation wastes time when you are writing or causes other trouble later.

If you are writing for someone else or if you are producing a document with many contributors (the state budgeting case illustrates both), remember to consult with others as needed to answer the questions.

STEP 1: Prepare

First, ask questions about the policy process.

Policy

- To what policy action (underway or anticipated) does this communication relate?
- Does a policy already exist?

Problem

- What conditions are problematic?
- What problem do these conditions present?
- How do I define the problem?
- How do others define the problem?

Actors

- Who are the actors?
- What are their roles?
- What are their interests?
- Who else has a significant role or interest in the process?

Politics

- What are the major disagreements or conflicts?
- What are the major agreements or common interests?
- Which actors are most likely to influence the process or the outcome?

STEP 2: Plan
Second, ask questions about the communication.

Purpose

- Why is this communication needed?
- What do I want to accomplish?

Message

- What is my message?
- How does my message differ from others on the topic?
- What argument will I make to support my message?
- How does my argument relate to others on the topic?

Role

- What is my role in this process?
- What is my interest in the outcome?

Authority
- Whose name will be on the document(s): Mine? Another's? An organization's?
- For whom does the communication speak?

Reception
- Who is (are) the named recipient(s)?
- Who will use the information?
- Will the document(s) be forwarded? Circulated? To whom? Represented? By whom?

Response
- What will recipients know after reading the document(s)? What will users of its information do?
- What is likely to happen as a consequence of this communication?

Setting and Situation
- What is the occasion? What is the time frame for communicating?
- Where, when, and how will this communication be presented?
- Where, when, and how will it be received? Used?

Form and Medium
- Is there a prescribed form, or do I choose?
- What is the appropriate medium for presentation and delivery? A written document? A telephone call? Email?

Contents
- What information will support the message?
- Where will a succinct statement of the message be placed?
- How should the contents be arranged to support the message?
- How will the document's design make information easy to find?

Tone and Appearance

- How do I want this communication to sound? What attitude do I want to convey?
- How do I want the document(s) to look? Is a style or layout prescribed, or do I choose how to present the contents?

Document Management

- Who will draft the document? Will there be collaborators?
- Who will review the draft? Who will revise it?

STEP 3: Produce

Based on your preparation and planning, write the document. Do it in three separate passes: draft first, review second, and revise third. Do not mix the tasks. Separating those tasks allows you to manage your time and handle distractions while you write, and to communicate better in the end.

The tasks are outlined here. Use this outline to stay on track if you're working alone, or under pressure, or producing a short document. If you're collaborating or team-writing, or if you're creating a multidocument product (such as the budget described in chapter 1), adapt the task outline to your circumstances.

Draft

- Produce a complete working draft in accordance with your preparation and plan (your answers to the questions above).

Review

- Compare the draft to the plan and highlight any differences.
- Get additional review of the draft by others, if advisable.
- Refer to the checklists (shown below) to assess the draft's effectiveness and quality and to highlight needs for revision.

Revise

- Make the changes called for by review.

Two Checklists

Features of Effectiveness. A public policy communication is most likely to be useful if it addresses a specific audience about a specific problem, has a purpose related to a specific policy action, represents authority accurately, uses the appropriate form, and is designed for use.

☐ Addresses a specific audience about a specific problem: In policy work, time is scarce. Specifying a communication's audience or intended recipient(s) and the subject or problem(s) saves thinking time for writer and reader (or speaker and listener). The information's relevance for the recipient should be made clear.

☐ Has a purpose related to a specific policy action: Policy cycles have several phases. Multiple actions and cycles are underway simultaneously. Timing matters. Agendas change. Stuff happens. Therefore, explicitly stating a communication's purpose and relevance to the recipient makes it more likely to get timely attention.

☐ Represents authority accurately: Policy communications do more than present information; they also represent a type of participation and power. For a policy communication to be taken seriously, to have influence, and to influence rightly, the communicator's role and status—a citizen with an opinion, an expert with an opinion, a spokesperson for a non-governmental organization, a government official—must be accurately represented.

☐ Uses appropriate form: Settings of policy work have their own conventions for communicating. Use the document type, style, and tone of presentation that are expected for the purpose and that accommodate working conditions in the setting of its reception.

☐ Is designed for use: People's attention is easily distracted in settings of policy work. Dense, disorganized text will not be read or heard. For people to comprehend under conditions of time pressure and information overload, contents must be easy to find and to use. Written documents should chunk information, use subheadings, and organize details in bulleted lists or paragraphs or graphics. Spoken texts should cue listeners' attention with similar devices.

Measures of Excellence. No two communications are exactly alike, but every public policy communication should try to meet criteria for clarity, correctness, conciseness, and credibility.

- ☐ Clarity: The communication has a single message that intended recipients can find quickly, understand easily, recognize as relevant, and use.

- ☐ Correctness: The communication's information is accurate.

- ☐ Conciseness: The communication presents only necessary information in the fewest words possible, with aids for comprehension.

- ☐ Credibility: A communication's information can be trusted, traced, and used with confidence.

Summary and Preview

Multiple actors in varied roles do policy work. They recognize the significance of communication in the process. Distilled into a general method for practical writing and speaking, their working knowledge of the process and communication's power can guide you to think about the fundamentals whenever you participate in a policy making process. Those fundamentals are role (who am I? what is my authority?); genre (what type of document or talk should I create?); purpose (what do I want to accomplish?); message (what do I want to say?); audience and reception (to whom, under what circumstances?); medium (how should I convey this message?); and effect (what might happen as a result of this communication?). This method keeps you on track, enables you to produce under pressure and to behave ethically, and supports accountability. Use it to write a problem definition in chapter 3, next.

Further Reading

Allison, L., and M. F. Williams. 2008. *Writing for the government*. The Allyn & Bacon Series in Technical Communication. New York: Pearson Longman.

Svara, J. 2007. *The ethics primer for public administrators in government and nonprofit organizations*. Sudbury, MA: Jones and Bartlett Publishers.

~~⌐◦

Definition:
Frame the Problem

Key Concepts

- Advocacy to get a problem on the public agenda
- Analysis of solutions
- Persuasion

This chapter applies communication and rhetoric principles to the definition of policy problems and the analysis of policy solutions.

How does public policy making begin? Typically, it starts with perception of a problem. Somebody perceives a condition in society or the environment to be wrong. Perceptions of a problem differ, so finding a solution often involves conflict. Or, it might enable cooperation.

Problems come to public attention in various ways. Sometimes the problem chooses you. Something happens, you are affected by it, and you seek public action to address the problem. The triggering event might be large scale, as when the destructive hurricanes Katrina and Rita damaged American coastal cities and states in 2005. After those storms, families of victims, local governments, and other collectives sought compensation or other action by federal government. In contrast, a triggering event might be small scale, even personal and singular. Following her child's death owing to a drunk driver, a parent formed the national nonprofit organization Mothers Against Drunk Driving to influence national law enforcement standards for drunk driving.

Sometimes you choose the problem. Choosers vary. For example, elected and appointed officials in government have authority to decide what is and is not a problem and which problems will receive attention. In the budgeting case (chapter 1), a governor and state legislative committees exemplify this kind of chooser. The food labeling case (chapter 1) shows an agency head choosing milk for a regulatory agenda. Outside government, a chooser might be an advocacy group or a coalition of groups that brings a problem to legislative attention.

To influence policy making, the perception of a wrong is not enough. If public policy is to be a solution, the wrong must be defined as one that policy makers can address. For example, you might perceive that obesity is wrong because it harms individuals, but individual solutions cannot be legislated. However, if you define obesity as a public health problem, you can relate obesity to public health standards or to medical research in the causes of disease. Those are problems with broad societal significance that can be addressed by policy makers.

Problem definition is important. As the logical first move in a policy process, problem definition sets debate; it also predicts solution. You point to a solution by the way you define the problem. Different definitions lead to different solutions. For example, even though health authorities define obesity as a health problem, the numbers of overweight and obese people especially in the United States continue to rise. Why, you wonder, are people fat despite health warnings? Your question redefines the problem, thereby revealing different potential solutions. By focusing on the experience of people in everyday life, you expose another set of conditions relevant to obesity, behavioral issues such as eating habits, physiological issues such as genetics, cultural issues such as food preferences, economic conditions such as food costs, and economic interests such as food industry profits. You point to solutions involving consumers, educators, businesses, and industries rather than healthcare providers.

Problem definition takes differences of perception into account. To a large degree, problem definition is subjective. One constituency's problem is another's acceptable status quo. Narrow and exclusive problem definition freezes possibility and invites competing solutions. Broad and inclusive definition imagines change and invites solution by a coalition. Rhetorical awareness (who am I? whom do I address? how do I define the problem? how do others define it? what other definitions are possible?) brings assumptions and values to light, creates awareness of difference, and enables negotiation.

No matter how messy the process becomes, your action in a policy process is directed by your definition of the problem.

How to Define a Policy Problem

Two purposes for defining a problem are differentiated in this chapter, getting an unrecognized problem on the public agenda by advocacy (Purpose A) and, for a recognized problem, aiding policy choice by analysis of solutions (Purpose B). Arguably, to cover two purposes in a single chapter confuses the goal, problem definition. From the perspective of a policy cycle, defining is not solving. Yet, from the perspective of communication in the process, defining and solving share an important characteristic, purposeful persuasion. Problem definition for any purpose is inherently rhetorical or persuasive (Stone 2002). Thus, two purposes are taught here: to differentiate between advocacy and analysis and to highlight the demand for rhetorical awareness in problem definition.

In practice, when you are defining a problem for policy work, know your purpose. For effective and ethical communication, knowing your purpose matters as much as knowing your audience.

Goal: Ability to recognize problematic conditions and to define a policy problem they present. For a recognized problem, ability to define policy options and to offer criteria for decision.

Objective: Problem definition.

Scope: Individual or collective; local or broader in impact; well known or unrecognized; widely discussed or little considered; past, present, or anticipated.

Strategy: Provide information necessary for your purpose.

Expect to be flexible in the writing process. Problem definition can be iterative. After completing a task, you might find that you must revise earlier work. Or, after defining a problem, you might find that you want to, or you must, redefine it because conditions have changed or you have gained more knowledge.

Purpose A: Get a Problem on the Public Agenda by Advocacy

You want to bring public attention to a problem of concern to you. It might be known to others, but only recently familiar to you. Or you might be aware of a problem of which others are unaware. In any case, you must understand the problematic conditions well.

To develop your understanding, follow an approach of observation and inquiry. Do the tasks below in sequence. Results of one task will help you perform the next one. Note: This task outline assumes that you are a novice in problem definition.

Task #1. Describe the problem and identify the stakeholders

First, describe the problem and name the interested parties, or stakeholders. This involves recognizing problematic conditions, identifying the problem that those conditions create, and specifying individuals as well as collectives that have a stake in the problem or its solution. To increase your awareness of problematic conditions and to recognize interests in it, you can proceed in any of the following ways:

- Work from observation of experiences, practices, effects:
  - Note likes/dislikes about your (or others') daily routine.
  - List good/bad aspects of your current or past job(s) or a family member's or a friend's job(s).
  - Sit for an hour in the office of a service provider to observe people affected by the problem and to observe the practices of policy implementers.
  - Visit locales affected by the conditions or the policy to observe impacts on physical environments.
- Work from subjective constructions:
  - Listen to or read stories (actual or imagined) that refer to the problem.
- Work from unfinished business:
  - Reexamine a neglected need.
  - Revive a former interest.
  - Return to an incomplete project.

- Work from anticipation:
  - Imagine the consequences if particular things continue as they are.
- Work from ignorance:
  - Choose a matter that concerns others (but is unfamiliar to you) that you want to know more about.
- Work from knowledge:
  - Consider the concern technically, informed by your (or others') expertise.
- Work from values:
  - Consider the concern ethically or legally, informed by your (or others') ideals or commitments.

Task #2. Specify the issues

When a problem has been identified, it is not yet a policy matter until its issues for policy are specified. Issues refer to stakeholders' concerns, political disagreements, and value conflicts. To recognize issues, you might do the following:

- Think about impacts of the problem. Who or what is affected by it?
- Conceive the problem narrowly and then broadly. Is it individual and local or more widespread?
- Conceive the problem broadly and then narrowly. Is it widely distributed or concentrated?
- Think about attitudes. How do different stakeholders perceive the problem? What values (ideals, beliefs, assumptions) are expressed in their definitions?
- Think about authority. How do stakeholders want to address the problem? Do they see government action as a solution? Do they agree or disagree on government's role?

Task #3. Offer solutions (if you are proposing a solution)

Solutions typically rely on policy instruments that government can use (Bardach 2005). These include actions such as spending more or spending less and starting or ending programs. If you already have a positive and feasible solution to suggest, do so. (Generally, problem descriptions with a proposed solution get more attention.) If you don't have a proposal, if you want to counter a proposal, or if you want to create fresh alternatives, stimulate your thinking with any of the following approaches:

- Review the problematic conditions with a fresh eye, looking for unnoticed solutions.
- Reconsider a tried-but-failed or a known-but-ignored solution to find new potential.
- Look at the problem from a different perspective (a different stakeholder's, for example).
- Assign it to a different governmental level or jurisdiction if government already addresses the problem.
- Consult with nonprofit groups and nongovernmental organizations that are concerned about the problem.
- Consider doing nothing (keep things as they are).

Task #4. Write the document: problem description

Before you write, use the Method (chapter 2) to make yourself aware of the rhetorical framework (audience, purpose, context, situation) for your communication. Write with that framework in mind.

Problem descriptions can be presented in varied document types. If the type is prescribed for you, use it in accordance with your rhetorical framework. If you are free to choose the document type, choose one that fits your audience, purpose, context, and situation. Here are two options:

1. Letter, memorandum, or report describing problematic conditions, possibly identifying causes of the conditions.
2. Letter, memorandum, or report conveying informed opinion, possibly advocating an approach to the problem.

Below, here, you can see memoranda written by professionals who are also graduate students and a report written by professionals. For letters, go to these respected sources:

- *CQ Weekly Report*, *CQ Researcher* available in print in subscribing libraries or online at http://library.cqpress.com
- Opinion sections of national newspapers such as the *New York Times* (http://www.nytimes.com), *Los Angeles Times* (http://www.latimes.com), *Chicago Sun-Times* (http://www.suntimes.com), or *Washington Post* (http://www.washpost.com)

Problem descriptions in any form are expected to answer the following questions:

- What are the problematic conditions? What problem do they cause?
- What are the issues for policy?
- What is your concern? What is your intended reader's concern?
- Who else is concerned (on all sides)?
- What are the key disagreements and agreements among those concerned?
- (optional) What plausible and realistic solution can you offer?

You must cite the sources to which your problem description refers. Use the citation style prescribed, or choose either the American Psychological Association (APA) style (described at http://www.apastyle.org/styletips.html) or the Modern Language Association (MLA) style (described at http://www.mla.org/style). Both APA and MLA style guides tell you how to cite a range of source types including government documents. (For example, see *Citing Government Information Sources Using MLA Style* at http://www. knowledgecenter.unr.edu/subjects/guides/government/cite.html.) For further help with citing government sources, consult Garner and Smith's (1993) *The Complete Guide to Citing Government Information Resources: A Manual for Writers and Librarians* (rev. ed.).

After you write, check your document's quality against the checklists in chapter 2.

Three Examples with Scenarios

Here, below, are three writing samples of problem definition for Purpose A. Preceding scenarios put them in context.

Scenario 1 (Purpose A—Get a Problem on the Public Agenda)

A graduate student of policy writing also serves professionally as the Chief of Patient Information in the Surgeon General's Office, U.S. Reserve Armed Forces. In her government workplace, she is the subject matter expert for clinical policy questions relating to health care eligibility and benefits, records administration, medical readiness, and associated Army policies and regulations. She conducts analyses to answer questions in her subject areas and writes policy documents. Regarding health care eligibility, a problematic condition has caught her attention. While doing routine research to answer an eligibility question, she finds that reserve component soldiers are not eligible for many of the medical and dental benefits available to active component soldiers.

Senior administrative officers have long been aware of this condition and they know that increased reserve deployments are worsening it. Senior administrators defined the benefits gap as a policy problem. They recommended a legislative solution involving changes to the Department of Defense's health program, but the recommendation was not accepted.

This problem known to others but not, until recently, to her becomes a focus of her graduate coursework. She utilizes an assignment to write a preliminary description of the problem as an informal memo (Example 1, below). Anticipating that she might be asked to communicate with policy makers if senior officers renewed their policy reform effort, she utilizes another coursework opportunity to draft a memo to the chair of a Congressional subcommittee with jurisdiction (Example 2, below). At this point, these memos inform only the writer; they serve to exercise arguments for advocacy.

Example 1. (*Purpose A—Get a Problem on the Public Agenda*)

Memorandum

To: (Primary Audience—Still being determined)

Cc: (Secondary Audience—Still being determined)

From: (Author)

Date: (Date of publication)

Subject: Expansion of Healthcare Benefits for Reserve Component Service Members

Overview of the Problem

Three hundred thousand American citizens serve in the Reserve Armed Force (RAF), with the number increasing daily. Even though the Reserved Armed Force has devoted over 60 million man-days to the Global War on Terror, these Soldiers do not receive the same medical or dental benefits as their Active Component (AC) counterparts. Due to the different lifestyle of a Reserve Component (RC) Soldier compared to an AC Soldier and the varying benefits, Reserve Armed Force units are struggling to meet medical readiness goals for worldwide deployments and operations.

Causes of the Problem

Current Operations Tempo: The current operational tempo of the United States military requires both AC and RC units to deploy on regular and frequent rotations. The RAF was established with a 5:1 ratio of training to operational years of service. Currently, most RAF units are barely meeting a 2:1 ratio. The lack of dwell time between deployments requires soldiers to maintain a much higher level of constant medical readiness.

Lack of Outside Health Insurance/Financial Hardship: While the majority of RAF Soldiers have civilian employment, the percentage with personal health insurance drops to less than 30% of the force. Even though enlistment contracts require Soldiers to maintain their medical readiness, many do not have personal insurance or the financial means to procure Healthcare.

Socioeconomic Status: RAF Soldiers have an average annual income that is 50% less than the average Air National Guard service member. While the "Hometown Recruiting" program has reached small communities and rural areas previously untapped for military service, the majority of the resulting force consists of blue-collar or farm-dependent citizens with a lower than average socioeconomic status.

Impact of the Problem

With the RAF quickly developing into an operational force, the United States depends on its service members to maintain a high state of medical readiness in preparation for worldwide deployments and missions. The lack of consistent healthcare benefits for RC Soldiers results in a national average of 23% Fully Medically Ready (FMR) Soldiers across the RAF. As a result, units are deploying to combat theaters with 10–15% fewer Soldiers than missions require. The resulting holes in coverage in security forces, logistics support, and medical providers in combat theaters are devastating the war fight and endangering the Soldiers that are able to fight, as they do not have the support they require.

Potential Solutions

Maintain Current System: Maintaining the current policy of 90 days of healthcare benefits prior to arrival at mobilization station will alleviate a small portion of the medical and dental issues preventing Soldiers from deploying. The current system balances the cost of healthcare with the cost of "fixing" a Soldier. This system does not allow for the deployment of Soldiers with issues that are treatable, yet require more than 60–90 days for optimum medical care.

Full Coverage for Alert: Soldiers currently receive full healthcare benefits 90 days prior to their arrival at the mobilization station. While this allows for them to receive care for minor illnesses and annual appointments, it does not allow enough time for Soldiers to receive treatment for more serious, yet treatable illnesses, such as hypertension, gum disease, or dental issues requiring dentures. Extending full healthcare coverage to Soldiers immediately upon alert of the unit will allow for the treatment of 95% of all dental issues, and the majority of illnesses which do not otherwise disqualify for worldwide deployment.

Full Coverage throughout Period of Service: Extending full healthcare benefits to RC Soldiers (which would mirror the full Tricare coverage AC Soldiers receive) would allow Soldiers to maintain a healthier lifestyle through regular medical and dental appointments. The potential gains of preventive medicine would, over time, reduce the cost of reactionary medicine for RC Soldiers, resulting in higher readiness rates. Additionally, if healthcare costs were covered, Soldiers could be held accountable for their individual medical readiness under statutes of the Uniform Code of Military Justice.

Next Steps

As the country continues to call upon our Reserve Component forces, it is critical that we establish a more thorough and dependable system of providing healthcare to RAF Soldiers. The discrepancy between benefits received by the AC and RC is monumental, despite the valiant service of both components on the battlefield. I challenge concerned citizens, leaders, and politicians to recognize the time and money being lost on professionally trained Soldiers who are unable to deploy due to preventable medical and dental issues. Disagreement with our country's position in the current war is unrelated to the benefits our Soldiers deserve for their service. Let us take care of the very men and women who are risking their lives for our country on the dangerous frontlines of the Global War on Terror by improving healthcare benefits regardless of duty status or military component.

Example 2. (*Purpose A—Get a Problem on the Public Agenda*)

To: Chair, Senate Armed Services Personnel Subcommittee

From: Military Healthcare Advocates Association

Date: March 25, 2008

Re: Expansion of Defense Health Program and Applicable Legislation

Overview

The United States Reserve Armed Forces...have limited healthcare benefits under the current Defense Health Program. Unless serving in a mobilized status for more than thirty days, Soldiers are not provided with any medical or dental care at military expense. As a result of their lack of healthcare coverage, many Soldiers are not meeting medical readiness standards, which is directly impacting unit readiness and deployability. Due to the frequency with which Reserve Component units are deploying, it is critical the Defense Health Program be updated to better support this population of the Armed Forces. The purpose of this document is to inform you of the need for increased benefits for Reserve Component Soldiers. We respectfully request that your committee consider the impact of these findings and amend the current Defense Health Program to accommodate these new require-ments for Reserve Component forces.

Position

An addition to the Defense Health Program that allows for full health-care benefits for Reserve Component Soldiers would result in higher rates of medical readiness, produce a more ready and deployable force, and ultimately serve as a retention tool.

Army medical readiness standards require all Soldiers to have a current physical exam, dental exam, vision screening, and applicable age or gender appropriate wellness exams. Together, these build a Soldier's "Individual Medical Readiness (IMR)" rate. Soldiers who are offered healthcare coverage are more likely to have regular wellness exams. Additionally, regular exams and care will result in a higher state of medical readiness, as unresolved issues are less likely to exist. Certain medical issues, such as high blood pressure, are easily rem-edied with medication, but require time to ensure accurate dosage and response to medication. Units could be unable to deploy a Soldier due to a simple illness, which could be avoided if the condition was receiv-ing regular monitoring and treatment. Full healthcare benefits would allow Soldiers to approach healthcare from a preventive standpoint, rather than simply reacting to sudden illnesses or injuries. Additionally, as the rate of Post-Traumatic Stress Disorder increases, full healthcare benefits will serve as a safety net to our Reserve Component Soldiers by giving them the means and ability to seek mental health assistance on their own terms. This preventive approach will decrease the rate of adjustment disorders following deployments, while offering support to families and communities upon their Soldier's return.

In addition to increasing IMR rates, full healthcare benefits would serve to increase unit readiness rates. Current policies do not provide leadership with the authority to hold Reserve Component Soldiers accountable for IMR failures, which is evident in the less than 20% IMR rate maintained by the average Reserve Component Soldier and which results in unit averages of 10–12% medically ready Soldiers (Sproat). If Soldiers are provided with healthcare coverage at government expense, commanders will have the legal authority to require Soldiers to maintain appropriate IMR rates. By empowering leaders to hold their Soldiers accountable, we are ensuring a more medically ready force through command emphasis and support.

As units maintain higher levels of medical readiness, leaders can reduce readiness exercises and minimize the time required to prepare for mobilization. Shorter mobilizations are healthier for families, and result in happier Soldiers and family members. As we reduce the Soldier's time away from his family, full healthcare benefits simultaneously allow a Soldier to better utilize his personal finances for family needs by removing the burden of paying for healthcare. This ultimately helps retain our Soldiers, who will be receiving quality care while providing for their families more completely.

In 2006 alone, seven units were extended in combat due to the failure of medical readiness standards on the part of their replacement unit, while the average 3,000-man unit returned 5% of their Soldiers from the mobilization station for failure to meet medical readiness standards (Sproat). Not only does this amount to countless hours of lost training, funding, and man hours for each returned Soldier, but it also constitutes a Soldier who will receive a last minute alert to report for duty as a replacement for the returned Soldier. The Reserve Components account for a mere 0.9% of the current Defense Health Program (H.R. 4986). An amendment to the plan to include full healthcare benefits for the Reserve Components would increase the overall cost of the program by approximately 5%, or $17 million (Sproat). This cost would be minimal compared to the cost of retaining a unit in a deployed theater due to last minute medical readiness failures or to conducting last minute training for a replacement Soldier.

While Reserve Component Soldiers are not serving in the military in a full-time capacity, all serve tours of Active Duty for combat deployments, homeland defense, or state emergencies. Their contribution to the nation's safety cannot be minimized because of their Reserve status. They make sacrifices in the same selfless manner as Active Duty Soldiers, and their sacrifices can often include extended time away from their family, combat tours or sustaining tragic injuries. Increased benefits would show our Reserve Component Soldiers our appreciation for their time, sacrifice, and service.

Regardless of the variety of opinions about the Global War on Terror, our Reserve Component servicemen and women deserve the support of their nation. Their sacrifices both overseas and in their hometowns make them heroes of the greatest caliber. Increasing the Defense Health Program to include full healthcare coverage for Reserve Component Soldiers would be an expression of gratitude for their continued service to our country. I urge you to consider the message you would send to the nation through this gesture of support for our troops.

Works Cited

"10 USCS § 1076d: Medical and Dental Care." (Current through 1/8/08). Text from *Code of Federal Regulations.* Available from Lexis Nexis® Congressional; Accessed 9 February 2008.

Chu, David S.C. Quote from: United States. Cong. Hearing of Senate Armed Services Personnel Subcommittee. "Military Personnel and Readiness; Reserve and Health Affairs." (Date: 3/28/2007). Text from Tricare Management Activity. Available from: <http://www.tricare.mil/planning/congress/downloads/ 20070407/03−28-07%20SASC-P%20Chu-Jones.pdf> Accessed 10 February 2008.

"History of TRICARE." 4 January 2007. <http://www.tricare.mil/mybenefit/ProfileFilter.do;jsessionid=H4vfbgT6TGFRd5kqSMYcQTNStCGQWnXyqqJHHQLbQdLpQf2v4qvz!1209655901?puri=%2Fhome%2Foverview%2FWhatIsTRICARE%2FHistory> Accessed 10 February 2008.

Sproat, David B. Personal Interview. 23 January 2008.

United States. Cong. House of Representatives, 110th Congress, 2nd Session. H.R. 4986. National Defense Authorization Act for Fiscal Year 2008 [introduced in the U.S. House of Representatives; 3 January 2008]. 110th Congress. Congressional Bills, GPO Access. 11 February 2008. <http://frwebgate.access.gpo.gov/cgibin/useftp.cgi?IPaddress=162.140.64.183&filename=h4986enr.txt&directory=/diska/wais/data/110_cong_bills>.

United States. Cong. House of Representatives, 109th Congress, 1st Session. H.R. 1815. National Defense Authorization Act for Fiscal Year 2006 [introduced in the U.S. House of Representatives; 26 April 2005]. 109th Congress. Congressional Bills, GPO Access. 9 February 2008.

What these examples show. Examples 1 and 2 on military health care benefits answer some, but not all, of the substantive questions for a problem description (Purpose A, Task #4). Both examples specify problematic conditions and identify the problem those conditions present, along with associated issues. Example 1 offers solution options. This is appropriate for the genre, problem description with proposed solutions but no recommendation. Example 2 argues for a single solution, again appropriately for its genre, memo advocating a solution intended to persuade a reader who has power to decide. Unanswered questions (Purpose A, Task #4) are the main weakness in both documents. Neither says who else is interested in the problem and what their likely disagreements or agreements might be. This weakness makes both descriptions less helpful to the writer for developing argumentation and finding a feasible solution.

This graduate student and government professional chose a written memorandum or memo as the medium of presentation. (Method, Step 2, chapter 2) This well-established genre of professional communication in the United States derived from the inverted pyramid of news writing. (In colonial America, it was called a memorial, meaning information to be remembered.) A memo is designed to be quickly read, easily understood and recalled, and easily referenced in discussion. Its compact form fits the time, attention, and accountability demands of governmental workplaces.

At the document's beginning, a stacked list identifies the communication's who (sender and addressed recipient), what (subject), why (purpose), and when (transmittal date). Other intended recipients might be specified in a "cc" ("copied on this communication") list placed either in the heading or at the document's end. The memo's text needs no title because its subject is identified in the heading by "re" ("regarding"). Text content is divided into sections with subheadings that cue readers as to the particulars covered in each section. In settings of policy work, this kind of organized, efficient document is preferred.

Examples 1 and 2 are presented here as written except for a name change. Capitalization ("S" in "Soldier") reflects prescribed writing style in the writer's workplace.

Scenario 2 (Purpose A—Get a Problem on the Public Agenda)

An attorney practicing civil law is also a graduate student of policy writing. He is concerned about the use of cell phones by drivers of cars. His concern arises in everyday experience, as he observed hazardous driving by people talking on cell phones. Given a coursework assignment to choose a perceived wrong and define it as a public policy problem, he chooses to define cell phone use while driving as a highway safety problem.

He uses assigned questions to prompt his recognition of emergent issues and to frame the problem. (See the questions in Purpose A, Task #4, this chapter.) To learn more about risks associated with using cell phones while driving, he searches for research publications in highway safety, public health, and related fields. To read argumentation about the risks, he searches for relevant policy analyses and judicial decision analyses. Thus prepared, he writes a preliminary problem description organized as answers to the prompting questions (Example 3, below). The answers synthesize his conception of the problem with pertinent research findings. At this point, the audience is the writer. Later, he will address a problem definition to legislative audiences.

Example 3. (Purpose A—Get a Problem on the Public Agenda)

Memo

To: (writer)

From: (writer)

Date: (X)

Re: Cell Phone Use While Driving is Unsafe

I. What are the problematic conditions? What problem do they present?

- The use of cell phones by drivers poses a significant safety threat
- The use of cell phones by drivers results in economic loss

The problematic condition in this area of inquiry is that the use of cell telephones by drivers creates a potential distraction, a distraction that could result in an accident with property damage and, more importantly, injury or death to motorists, their passengers or pedestrians. In a 2006 study of drivers in a driving simulator, professors at the University of Utah found that people are as impaired when they drive and talk on a cell phone as they are when they drive intoxicated at the legal blood-alcohol limit of 0.08 percent (Strayer, et al., 385–90). Specifically, these Utah researchers found that drivers that talked on a cell phone—hand-held or hands-free phones—"had slower reactions, had longer following distances, took longer to recover speed lost following a braking episode, and were involved in more accidents" (Strayer, et al., 388). In fact, their analysis "indicated that there were significantly more accidents when participants were conversing on a cell phone than in the baseline or alcohol conditions" (Strayer, et al., 388).

In addition to talking on a cell phone while driving, text messaging through a cell phone poses an even greater threat because it is not possible to use a "hands-free" device when texting.

The second problematic condition is the economic costs associated with the issue of a ban on cell phones while driving. Studies seem to conclude that the costs associated with banning cell phone use while driving are outweighed by the benefits. For example, a risk-benefit study by the Harvard Center for Risk Analysis found that "the cost of banning cell phone use while driving is about $700,000 for each quality-adjusted life year saved (Harvard Press Release). This same study found that a ban on the use of cell phones while driving is "30 times more expensive than achieving the same health benefit with driver airbags, and ten times more expensive than achieving the benefit by keeping the speed limit on interstate highways at 55 instead of 65 mph" (Harvard Press Release). Another study concluded that cell phone users would have to be compensated in excess of 41 billion dollars to be "indifferent" to a ban on cell phones while driving (Hahn, et al., 2). This dollar amount, then, was balanced against an annual death rate of approximately 300 people killed in accidents as a result of cell phone distraction (Hahn, et al., 4). However, while policy makers have to take into account these "costs" as defined by researchers, they must also be acutely aware that these abstract formulas can never adequately define or address the real value of a human life.

II. What are the issues for policy?

- Balance of individual right to use cell phone while driving versus state interests in safe and efficient roadways

- Any ban on cell phone use while driving could be difficult to enforce
- Potential negative political response by constituents to a criminal ban on the use of cell phones while driving
- Potential impact on civil actions involving claims of negligence in automobile accidents

The only issue here that needs further explanation is the idea of a potential impact on civil actions involving claims of negligence. In North Carolina, if a person breaks the law and, in so doing, causes an accident, then the law presumes that that person acted negligently. If not rebutted, then the only issue to be decided at trial is the amount of damages. (Carr v. Murrows Transfer, Inc.) Any legislation in this area would need to address this concept, that is, a policy could be implemented that provides that an infraction for the use of a cell phone while driving would or would not constitute negligence per se.

III. What is my concern?

- Highway safety

IV. Who else is concerned?

- Law enforcement
- Insurance industry
- Cell phone industry
- Automobile industry

The people likely to be concerned in this area are those most intimately tied to cell phones and drivers. Law enforcement and insurance companies have an interest in this area. Law enforcement personnel are the people on the forefront of this issue. When they respond to an accident, it is much more than a statistical evaluation; they have to deal with the real-life injuries and death that can occur as a result of inattentive driving. Also, insurance companies have an economic interest in reducing the number of accidents on our streets and highways. Certainly, companies that provide cell phone service have a vested interest in such legislation as it is likely to have a negative impact on their profits. Finally, automobile manufacturers are starting to incorporate hands-free phones into the cars they are manufacturing. State legislation that bans only the use of hands-held phones while driving could result in an upsurge in the demand for vehicles with built-in hands-free phones, while a ban on the use of any kind of cell phone while driving could diminish the amount of profit per vehicle manufactured with a built-in hands-free cell phone.

V. What are the key disagreements and agreements among those concerned?

- Key Agreements:
  - Distractions while driving can produce disastrous results
  - Safety on our streets and highways is an important consideration
- Key Disagreements:
  - Experienced drivers can talk on the cell phone while driving without posing a threat of danger to themselves or others
  - Benefits of a ban on cell phone use while driving are outweighed by the costs of such a policy
  - The use of hands-free cell phones while driving is an acceptable alternative

VI. What plausible and realistic solutions can I offer?

The solution being offered is to make the use of cell phones while driving illegal. In a perfect world, drivers would not be able to use any kind of cell phone while driving because I believe it is the lack of focus on the road that is so deadly, not the loss of one hand on the steering wheel. However, I believe that our country is headed towards banning only the use of hand-held cell phones while driving.

But, at this stage, I offer the following reasonable, if not realistically passed, solution. The use of any kind of cell phone while driving would be an infraction, with a fine of up to $100 plus costs of court. This infraction would be reported to the Department of Motor Vehicles, but a first offense would not result in either points against the person's driver's license or in an insurance point. However, for every infraction after the first, drivers would receive 2 points on their driver's licenses and one insurance point as well. Finally, the following exceptions would be a part of my policy. Police, fire, and rescue personnel, including public and private ambulance drivers are exempted from this law, and any person can use a cell phone while driving in an emergency situation.

Works Cited

Carr v. Murrows Transfer, Inc., 262 N.C. 550, 138 S.E.2d 228 (1964).

Hahn, Robert, Paul Tetlock and Jason Burnett, "Should you be allowed to use your cellular phone while driving?" Regulation 23, No. 3. Online: 10

April   2008.   http://www.cato.org/pubs/regulation/regv23n3/hahn.pdf.
Accessed December 2, 2008.

Harvard School of Public Health. Press Release. "Study finds that restricting
cell phones while driving may be premature, that benefits may be more com-
pelling the with the risks." Accessed April 3, 2008. http://www.hsph.harvard.
edu/news/press-releases/archives/2000-releases/press07242000.html.

Strayer, David, Frank Drews & Dennis Crouch. "A comparison of the cell phone
driver and the drunk driver." Human Factors 48 (Summer 2006): 381–391.

What this example shows. The strength of Example 3 on drivers' cell
phone use is its focus on defining the problem. As noted earlier in
this chapter, problem definition is subjective. This writer articulates
his answer to the central question, what is the problem? He suggests
a plausible solution, but he does not attempt to offer alternatives and
grounds for decision.

Another strength is the specification of the cultural context for
engaging this problem (Method, Step 1, chapter 2). The writer identifies actors, roles, and interests along with their agreements and
disagreements. The writer clearly distinguishes his own interest as a
citizen and the public's interest from special interests.

As a policy communication, however, this problem description is
not ready for actual use. Like earlier samples that served as thinking
pieces for a professional, Example 3 serves as a thinking exercise for
a citizen. Nonetheless, the document meets some criteria for communication effectiveness and excellence in policy work settings. It
accurately represents the authority of an informed citizen. Its bulleted list organization meets time demands of harried policy makers.
Its single message can easily be located. Its synthesis of information
sources, carefully cited, demonstrates credibility.

Wordiness weakens this communication. Especially, sentences
typically run long and repeat ideas. Busy readers might soon start
reading selectively or hunting for nuggets of information. Occasional
short summary sentences, placed strategically, could guide readers to
the writer's key points.

A good next step for this writer would be to turn the problem
description into a one-pager, a popular genre in policy-work settings.
The organization here, particularly the bulleted lists followed by text

explanation, easily translates to a one-pager. Text can be condensed to essential claims. Supporting detail can go into an accompanying oral briefing or a supplemental document available if requested. References can be supplied if requested.

Purpose B: Aid Policy Choice by Analysis of Solutions

A problem is recognized. Policy alternatives for addressing it are under consideration. You are asked or you wish to present a definition of the problem and a review of policy alternatives. Your intended audience might be policy makers, an interested community, or the general public. Follow a strategy of formal analysis using quantitative or qualitative methods. (Note: The task outline assumes that you are prepared to perform—outside the tasks listed here—appropriate technical analysis needed to answer the questions.)

Task #1. Identify the problem and the stakeholders

- What is the problem? What brings it to attention?
- Why does the problem occur? What conditions lead to it?
- Whose behavior is affected, or whose concerns are relevant? Who are the target beneficiaries of solutions to the problem? Who are the implementers of policy to solve it?
- What stake does each (affected groups, target beneficiaries, implementers of policy) have in the problem?
- How does each define the problem?
- What ideals and values (equity, liberty, efficiency, security, loyalty) or ideologies (vision of how the world is or how it should be) are expressed in each definition?
- What conflicts of values or ideologies are evident among stakeholders?
- How does politics influence the problem?

Task #2. Specify alternative solutions and relevant criteria for evaluating them

- What are the goals/objectives of a public policy to solve this problem?

- What policy instruments might achieve the goals/objectives?
- What are at least two (alternative) policies to meet the need?
- What are the relevant criteria for choosing the best one? How do stakeholders weigh the criteria? How appropriate are the weights? What are the trade-offs among criteria?
- What would be the outcome of each alternative according to criteria you consider relevant?

Task #3. Recommend an alternative and explain your reasoning (if you are making a recommendation)

- Which policy option or instrument do you recommend? Why is it best? Why are other alternatives worse?
- What is the basis for your recommendation? What type of analysis supports it?
- How will your choice affect stakeholders?
- On what conditions (political, economic, organizational) does successful implementation of your choice depend?
- What are the constraints (political, economic, organizational) on implementing your choice?

Task #4. Write the document: policy analysis with (or without) recommendation

Before you write, use the Method (chapter 2) to consider your communication rhetorically and to plan it. After you write, use the checklists (chapter 2) to assess the document and revise as needed.

Policy analysis is communicated in varied document types. If a particular type is prescribed for you, use it in accordance with your intended purpose and audience. Policy studies courses might prescribe a policy analysis memo, for instance. If you are free to choose, you might use either a memo or an extended discussion paper.

Policy analyses in any form are expected to

- characterize a problem according to its size, scope, incidence, effects, perceptions of it, and influences on it;
- identify policy choices available to address the problem;
- offer perspectives to assist choice making;
- specify the basis for selecting any proposed recommendation (the type of analysis performed), the effects for different groups, and the factors that will affect its implementation.

You must cite the sources to which your policy analysis refers. Use the citation style prescribed, or choose either the APA style (http://www.apastyle.org/styletips.html) or the MLA style (http://www.mla.org/style). Both APA and MLA style guides tell you how to cite a range of source types including government documents. (For example, see *Citing Government Information Sources Using MLA Style* at http://www.knowledgecenter.unr.edu/subjects/guides/government/cite.html.) For more help, consult Garner and Smith's (1993) *The Complete Guide to Citing Government Information Resources: A Manual for Writers and Librarians* (rev. ed.).

Two Examples

Here, below, are two examples of defining a recognized problem by analysis of solutions, Purpose B.

Example 4. (Purpose B—Aid Policy Choice)
Professional policy analysts wrote this brief with recommendations.

Expanding the EITC for Single Workers and Couples without Children (aka Tax Relief for Low-Wage Workers)

A Policy Brief prepared for the Center on Poverty, Work and Opportunity at the University of North Carolina at Chapel Hill

January 2007

Abstract
The Earned Income Tax Credit (EITC), the nation's largest anti-poverty program, now provides tax benefits of roughly $39 billion dollars a year to over 21 million households. By supplementing the earnings of low wageworkers, the EITC "makes work pay." The EITC's popularity can be attributed to its providing both work incentives and tax relief. In 1993, Congress extended a small earned income credit to single and childless couples; however, about 96 percent of EITC dollars still go to families with children. This discussion paper argues that, while the emphasis of the EITC on rewarding work for families with children deserves continued primacy, expansion of the EITC to childless single workers and married couples without children deserves greater attention for the following reasons:

- The disproportionate and growing income tax burden (payroll, sales, excise) faced by this group of workers;

- The growing segment of workers at the bottom of the labor market, particularly single men with low levels of education and training, who remain confined to low wage jobs;
- The strict separation in our thinking between households with and without children requires reexamination, given the growing number of children with non-custodial parents; and,
- With a national savings rate below zero, the need to facilitate asset building for all low-wage workers, including those without children.

We recommend expanding the EITC for single workers and childless married couples with a range of policy recommendations, each targeting specific new subgroups of EITC recipients and addressing a slightly different purpose:

1. Increase the EITC from 7.65 percent to 15.3 percent of earnings up to $8,080 in order to directly offset payroll taxes; and adjust the phase-in and phase-out ranges;

2. Lower the age requirement for single and childless workers to qualify for the EITC from 25 to 21 to target greater workforce participation incentives to young workers just entering the labor market and making major decisions about work;

3. Encourage single low-income workers to claim the Advance (monthly) EITC and use the increase in employee payroll earnings to contribute toward health care insurance premiums; and,

4. Link the EITC to asset building options such as matched savings accounts for education and training, homeownership, retirement, and entrepreneurship. In addition, remove asset limits for other public benefit programs, particularly to assist those with disabilities to enter the labor market and build assets.

Introduction

The Earned Income Tax Credit (EITC) is a refundable federal income tax credit first enacted with bipartisan political support in 1975. The EITC encourages low-income workers with children to enter and remain in the labor market by supplementing the earnings of those working for low wages, thus "making work pay."...In this policy brief, we explore three questions:

1. What do existing policy research and current data tell us about whether the original two goals of the EITC—payroll tax relief and encouraging employment—are being met adequately for the sub-groups of childless single and married workers;

2. Are there additional rationales that would justify an expansion of the EITC for this sub-group; and,

3. What policy changes could accomplish all or some of these policy goals?...

Summary of Key Findings

[Additional content omitted.]

- The disproportionate tax burden faced by low-wage single workers, which has worsened since the EITC was enacted in 1975, makes tax relief an even greater priority as an issue of tax fairness...If any workers need a tax cut, we argue that these workers do.

- A growing segment of workers at the bottom of the labor market...remain confined to low-wage jobs and earn marginal incomes or have dropped out of the labor market altogether...Leaving this group at the margins of the labor market undermines the strength of the workforce, communities, and families.

Additional Rationales for Expanding the EITC for "Childless" Workers:

In addition to the need for the EITC to better meet the goals of tax relief and encouraging work for childless workers, we also identified three additional reasons why an expansion of the EITC is warranted:

- Given changes in family structure and the growing number of children with non-custodial parents, the strict separation in our thinking between households with and those without children requires reexamination...

- Single workers who now qualify for the very modest credit can receive few if any other government benefits...

- With the national savings rate at zero, innovative approaches that promote savings and asset building for all low-income workers deserve support....

Policy Options for an Expansion of the EITC for Childless Workers

[Additional content omitted.]

Politically, at both the federal and state level, an expanded EITC could embody both progressive and conservative values by: (1) rewarding those who work with an earnings subsidy; (2) providing the greatest benefits to those with the greatest need; (3) offsetting the tax burden on working poor single and childless married couples struggling to make ends meet; (4) providing incentives for people to enter the workforce who otherwise might not do so; (5) achieving these ends without increasing employer costs, without creating hiring disincentives and with minimal government bureaucracy; and 6) helping single workers and families without children, and potentially many more, to build assets for homeownership, education, and retirement when combined with other institutional supports such as matched savings programs....

Analysis and Policy Proposals
[Additional content omitted.]

Conclusions and Suggestions for Policy Reform
[Additional content omitted.]
(The complete policy brief including footnotes, tables, charts, appendices, and references can be found at http://www.law.unc.edu/documents/poverty/publications/gittermanpolicybrief.pdf.)

What this example shows. This policy brief focuses on solving a recognized problem by a recommended solution, tax code reform. The authors define the problem narrowly as the need to extend a tax credit to more groups; however, their analysis of policy options for reforming the tax code and their recommendations invite broad political support.

This brief's strength is authoritative argumentation. (A logic outline of its policy argument is shown in chapter 5 on writing a position paper.) Organization is another strength. Despite its title "A Policy Brief" this 55-page document shows that policy communication is not always short. In longer documents subheadings are essential to keep readers on track. Previews at the start of each subsection provide orientation. They also give the authors an opportunity for making persuasive claims. Numbered or bulleted lists of discussion items help readers to remember—especially helpful for numeric or statistical information conveyed in text—and to find individual items quickly on referral later. Surrounded by "white space," the bulleted lists attract the reader's eye.

To some readers, this policy analysis might go too far toward advocacy. To decide for yourself, see another brief that is too lengthy to include here, a cost-effectiveness analysis of mandatory sentences for drug-related crimes prepared by the Rand Corporation and reprinted as Appendix A in *A Practical Guide to Policy Analysis* (Bardach 2005).

Example 5. *(Purpose B—Aid Policy Choice)*

This report describes a recognized problem and recommends a solution. Professional policy and program analysts in the U.S. Government Accountability Office, the auditing, research, and investigative staff of the Congress, wrote it. In a letter of transmittal not shown here, the authors address the report to the Chairman and Ranking Member, Committee on Armed Services, Senate and House of Representatives.

Defense Health Care

DOD Needs to Address the Expected Benefits, Costs, and Risks for Its Newly Approved Medical Command Structure

Highlights of GAO-08–122 (issued October 12, 2007), a report to congressional committees.

Why GAO Did This Study

The Department of Defense (DOD) operates one of the largest and most complex health systems in the nation and has a dual health care mission—readiness and benefits. The readiness mission provides medical services and support to the armed forces during military operations. The benefits mission provides health care to over 9 million eligible beneficiaries, including active duty personnel, retirees, and dependents worldwide. Past GAO and other reports have recommended changes to the military health system (MHS) structure. GAO was asked to (1) describe the options for structuring a unified medical command recommended in recent studies by DOD and other organizations and (2) assess the extent to which DOD has identified the potential impact these options would have on the current MHS. GAO analyzed studies and reports prepared by DOD's Joint/Unified Medical Command Working Group, the Defense Business Board, and the Center for Naval Analyses, and interviewed department officials.

What GAO Found

DOD considered options to address the department's dual health care mission that differed in their approaches to both command structure and operations. In April 2006, the Joint/Unified Medical Command

Working Group identified three options: (1) establishing a unified medical command on par with other functional combatant commands; (2) establishing two separate commands—a Medical Command, which would provide operational/deployable medicine, and a Healthcare Command, which would provide beneficiary health care through the military treatment facilities and civilian providers; and (3) designating one of the military services to provide all health care services across the department. Subsequently, in November 2006, a fourth option was presented that would consolidate key common services and functions, which are currently performed within each of the services, such as finance, information management and technology, human capital management, support and logistics, and force health sustainment. This option would leave the existing structures of the Army, Navy, and Air Force medical departments over all military treatment facilities essentially unchanged. The Deputy Secretary of Defense approved this fourth option in November 2006.

Although DOD initiated steps to evaluate the impact that some restructuring options might have on the MHS, it did not perform a comprehensive cost-benefit analysis of all potential options. GAO's Business Process Reengineering Assessment Guide establishes that a comprehensive analysis of alternative processes should include a performance-based, risk-adjusted analysis of benefits and costs for each alternative. The working group used several methods to determine some of the benefits, costs, and risks of implementing its three proposed options. For example, it used the Center for Naval Analyses to determine the cost implications for each option, and it solicited the views of key stakeholders. However, based on the working group's methodology, the group intended to conduct a more detailed cost-benefit analysis of whichever of the three options senior DOD leadership selected, but the group's work ceased once the fourth option was formally approved. While DOD approved the fourth option, DOD has not demonstrated that its decision to move forward with the fourth option was based on a sound business case. Based on GAO's review of DOD's business case, DOD has described only what it believes its chosen option will accomplish. The business case does not demonstrate how DOD determined the fourth option to be better than the other three in terms of its potential impact on medical readiness, quality of care, beneficiaries' access to care, costs, implementation time, and risks because DOD does not provide evidence of any analysis it has performed of the fourth option or a sound business case justifying this choice. Without such analysis and documentation, DOD is not in a sound position to assure the Secretary of Defense and Congress that it made an informed decision when it chose the fourth option over the other three or that its chosen option will have the desired impact on DOD's MHS.

What GAO Recommends

GAO is recommending that DOD address the expected benefits, costs, and risks for implementing the fourth option and provide Congress the results of its assessment. In commenting on a draft of this report, DOD concurred with GAO's recommendations.

This is a summary of the report. To view the full product, including the scope and methodology, go to http://www.gao.gov/new.items/d08122.pdf. For more information, contact Henry L. Hinton, Jr. at (202) 512–4300 or hintonh@gao.gov.

What this example shows. Example 5 exhibits many desirable qualities in public policy communication. Although its authors did not use the guidance offered here to compose it, the document exemplifies the qualities that this guide supports.

The report meets expected standards. It is intended for a specific audience whose particular information needs are identified in the document. It is clear, concise, and credible (checklists, chapter 2).

GAO is a respected governmental agency, so the document gains some credibility from its source. In addition, the writers have used design features that support the assessment that the document's information is credible (and thus presumed to be accurate). By stating explicitly for whom the report speaks (GAO), to whom it is addressed (a congressional committee chair who requested it), and who has reviewed it (DOD, the subject of the investigation), the report is accountable. Its authority is traceable.

Attention is paid to likely circumstances of the document's reception. The organization highlights key information and makes it easy to find on referral (important if the document will be circulated or summarized in a briefing). For example, a one-sentence statement of the message appears under the pointed subheading "What GAO Found." In the document as a whole, subheadings highlight key information by asking implicit questions that following information answers. The subheadings function as signposts pointing to the location of important information. Within subsections, the presentation moves in top-down or general-to-particular order, with summaries first and details second. These organizational devices help readers to read quickly and information users to find quickly what they need (see Method, chapter 2).

The genre is a report. Government agencies such as GAO often specify reports to be used for a purpose. In GAO's case, written reports are specified for communicating formal (finished) results of investigation requested by a Congress member. Institutions sometimes also prescribe a house style of document design. GAO style for report summaries, or the condensed abstract of a report, is illustrated here: three main sections (why the study was done, what was found, what is recommended) in prescribed layout. The summary ends with a locator for the full report and contact information for the report's author. These concluding devices add to the document's credibility.

Summary and Preview

This chapter tells you that problem definition is fundamental in policy work. Because problems can be defined differently, persuasive argumentation is a valuable skill. In chapter 4 you'll learn about conducting government records research to inform argument. In chapters 5 and 6 you'll learn about arguing in political contexts.

References

Bardach, E. 2005. *A practical guide for policy analysis: the eightfold path to more effective problem solving.* 2nd ed. CQ Press.

Garner, D. L., and D. H. Smith. 1993. *The complete guide to citing government information resources: a manual for writers and librarians.* Rev. ed. Bethesda, MD: Congressional Information Service.

Stone, D. 2002. *Policy paradox: the art of political decision making.* Rev. ed. New York: WW Norton & Company.

CHAPTER 4

Legislative History: Know the Record

Key Concepts

- Record of legislative action
- Legislative intent

Public policy making requires information about prior government action. This chapter shows you how to research legislative records and to write a legislative history.

Many kinds of information are needed for policy making. To frame a problem, identify its issues, or propose solutions, you might need to know about influential social history, technological developments, and economic patterns. You might consult scientific research, public testimony, advice of expert consultants and lobbyists, statistical data, government agency reports, transcripts of legal proceedings, and more. But one kind of information is essential: the history of government action on the problem. To get that information, you must consult the legislative record; you must be able to conduct legislative research using government documents.

Why is knowledge of the record important? Three reasons. First, for policy making, precedent matters. Action builds on prior action. Knowledge of precedent helps you to frame problems and to find solutions. Second, context matters. The record shows deliberation and debate. Third, content matters. The preamble or the statement of purpose of a published bill or law enables you to discern original intent and the intent of amendments. If you are proposing new action, credibility and standards for policy argument demand that you know the history of prior action.

Who conducts legislative research, and for what purposes? Government staff members (and sometimes interns) consult the legislative record to help them frame problems and identify issues. Outside government, professional staff (and sometimes interns) in organizations of many kinds such as nonprofit groups, trade associations, and policy institutes, consult the record. They do so in order to inform their advocacy or analysis. Similarly, active citizens consult the record as independent researchers. They might pursue a personal interest, or they might volunteer to investigate a record of action that is relevant to an organization's mission. For legal interpretation, court clerks, law librarians, and legal services professionals regularly consult the legislative record to know a law's intent as part of adjudicating disputes over a law's meaning.

Who writes legislative history documents? Often, the people who conduct the research also write the document that reports the results. Government staff or professional researchers on contract to a committee or agency or volunteers for organizations, as well as individuals doing independent research, might produce a legislative history tailored to a particular need to know.

Interns might be assigned these research and writing tasks. To illustrate, a supervisor in a health care policy institute asks an undergraduate intern to specify unmet needs in elder health care for a position paper being written by the institute's director. The supervisor gives no instructions on how to gather the necessary information. The intern considers how to approach the task. She figures that in order to identify unmet needs, she must know what current law provides. As a strategy for getting started, she works from familiar experience. Her elderly grandparents experienced nursing home care, so she decides to start by collecting information on nursing homes.

She goes, first, to the institute's reports published on its website. She finds that they are in-depth analyses of individual laws. Because the website has no index or search engine, she cannot locate laws that refer to nursing homes unless she reads all the reports. She does not have time for that. She then tries searching on the Internet, using an all-purpose search engine and the search term "nursing home care."

That yields advertisements for providers and websites of advocacy groups, but little legislation or public debate. Stymied, she asks the institute's professional staff for help. A policy analyst directs her to government databases and to commercial databases of government information on the Internet. She uses the indexing vocabulary for each database to streamline her searches by emerging topics—first, nursing home care; then hospital care, prescription drugs, and so on. Search results suggest to her that a good time frame to focus on would be the years in office of the previous federal government administration. She searches her favorite government database again in that time frame, and she spends several hours reading summaries of laws and proposed bills. She also checks the final action taken on each.

By the end of the day, she writes a two-page legislative history of elder care. She defines the most pressing current needs to be those that were recognized by the previous administration but left unresolved. She summarizes a list of unmet needs culled from a range of bills or amendments proposed but not passed or adopted. She identifies the most significant failures in elder healthcare proposals (according to criteria that she provides) and distills the public debate surrounding them. In a concluding reference list, she cites these bills or amendments by bibliographic identifiers in the databases so that the institute director can quickly find the acts to read their language. Task accomplished.

How to Conduct Legislative Research and Write a Legislative History

Goal: Knowledge of U.S. proposed or enacted law regarding a defined problem based on consulting legislative records.

Objective: Credible reporting of government action.

Product: Written document tracing either history of a single law or history of laws on an issue.

Scope: Either a single law or an issue involving multiple laws. Relevant action might be at the federal, state, or municipal level, or at several levels. In addition to legislative records, administrative records of rule making and regulation and judicial records of litigation might be needed.

Strategy: Multiple approaches are available. No single approach to government records research fits all; however, you will save time and frustration by planning before you start. Use the guidelines given in the following sections to select a strategy.

Know why the research is needed. Legislative uses for the research might be satisfied with past records. In contrast, legal uses might require very current information not yet recorded that only an informant can provide. Knowing the purpose for the research tells you what, and how much, to look for. Will the information be used to make new law (legislative) or to interpret existing law (legal)?

In either case, there might be a published history that meets the purpose. Or you might need to find the records required to write a specialized history. Knowing the purpose for the research can help you (or a librarian assisting you) to decide where to look first. Do you want to find a history or write one?

Know the user and the user's purpose for the information. Who, exactly, will use the information, and what is his or her interest or need? The user might be you, gathering information for personal use or for an academic or internship assignment. Or the user for whom you are conducting the research might be a legislator who wants to amend an existing law. Knowing the user's purpose tells you what, and how much, to look for. Federal records only? State or municipal records also?

Set the scope. Will the research follow a single law through all its forms and related actions—bill, codified statute, administration, regulation, amendment, and (possibly) adjudication? Or will your research follow an issue through policy changes and across multiple laws over time? What is the relevant time frame? What is the relevant level of government?

Take the necessary time, and manage your time. Records research can take hours, days, or weeks, depending on how much you already know, what you are looking for, where the records are, how well you have planned, and other contingencies. Prepare for the reality that legislative records research will take time, probably more time than you initially planned. What is your deadline for completing the research? What is your schedule for conducting the research and writing the necessary documents?

Use existing skills, and add needed ones. If you have a well-defined problem, are willing to learn, are curious and persistent, and have basic research skills including the ability to ask questions, identify relevant sources, and search computer databases, you are basically ready to perform legislative research.

You might need to learn about the legislative process, government record types, and standard tools for researching government records. If so, review as necessary using the tools suggested below.

Task #1. Review the legislative process

If you already know federal legislative procedure well or if you are tracing state law, omit Task #1 and go on to Task #2.

As you conduct research in government records, you can feel as if you are drowning in information, classification systems, procedure names, and document types. Also, if you start into records searching without knowing the underlying legislative process, you will quickly become lost. Use the following reviews of the process to revive your effort (bookmarking your favorite and returning to it as often as needed):

- The House: How Our Laws Are Made (by House of Representatives Parliamentarian) http://thomas.loc.gov/home/lawsmade.toc.html

- The Senate: Enactment of a Law (by Senate Parliamentarian) http://thomas.loc.gov/home/enactment/enactlawtoc.html

- The Legislative Process (by House of Representatives Information Office) http://www.house.gov/house/Tying_it_all.html

- The Legislative Process (by Indiana University Center on Congress) http://congress.indiana.edu/learn_about/topic/legislative_process.php

- The Legislative Process (by Capitol Advantage) http://congress.org/congressorg/issues/basics/?stylelegis

Task #2. Conduct research

Do you want to find a history or write one? Decide early whether your purpose is served by using an already published history or by producing one. For single laws, commercial research services such as the Congressional Information Service publish legislative histories with varying levels of detail. To look for a published history for a single law, try these sources:

- Law Librarians Society of Washington, D.C., Legislative Sourcebook http://www.llsdc.org/sourcebook

- CIS/Annual (Year), Legislative Histories of U.S. Public Laws

You are unlikely to find published legislative histories for an issue. They are typically produced by, or for, the people who want the information.

As a general rule, federal records are accessible online and in research libraries. State records are generally less so, but an individual state's records might be available online or, more likely, in the print archives of the state's library. Local government records are generally not available unless you go to the municipality to ask about access to records. Few municipalities put their records online.

Major tools for finding federal and state records are provided by government information services, either free or by subscription. Free services can be accessed from any computer with World Wide Web access. Subscription services are accessed via the Web by authorized users of facilities provided by a subscriber, such as a university library.

From your computer at home and in many public libraries, you can freely access federal records back to 1970 (and link to online state records) through:

- Thomas (Library of Congress) http://thomas.loc.gov

- Government Printing Office (GPO) Access http://www.gpoaccess.gov

Other free access to numerous federal government websites that link to records is provided by

- Federal Government Documents on the Web (University of Michigan Documents Center) http://www.lib.umich.edu/govdocs/federal.html

- U.S. Government Documents (Mansfield University) http://lib.mansfield.edu/gov-ref.cfm

- Catalogue of U.S. Government Publications http://catalog.gpo.gov/F

For state legislatures and local government, these are good websites:

- State and Local Governments (Library of Congress) http://www. loc.gov/rr/news/stategov/stategov.html
- Legal Research Guide-Government Resources (Virtual Chase) http://www.virtualchase.com/topics/government.shtml
- Law Librarians Society of Washington, D.C., Legislative Sourcebook: State Legislatures, State Laws, State Regulations http://www.llsdc.org/sourcebook

An excellent subscription service used in most university libraries for comprehensive federal legislative information is Lexis-Nexis *Congressional*, based on the (print) *Congressional Information Service* (CIS). This database is available to subscribers only. You can access it in subscribing research libraries. Free and subscription services are available in federal depository libraries. Those are research libraries, often at colleges and universities, that make GPO materials publicly available in the library's region. Find a depository library near you in the Federal Depository Library Locator at http:// www.gpoaccess.gov/libraries.html.

Libraries offer a valuable resource: librarians! For professional, skilled, and time-saving assistance in legislative research, always ask a librarian.

General Tips for Using Government Information Libraries

- Depository libraries have federal government records in all available forms—digital, print, and microfiche. Depending on what you want to know, you might need all three. Online access to digital records is convenient for recent records, but print and microfiche are still important, too, for several reasons. Records before the 1970s are not yet available online, and some never will be. You can miss a lot of legislative history if you only search online. Also, print compilations are sometimes easier to use, because they are well supplemented by indexes and other locator aids. When using a tool new to you, check first for finding aids, such as an index. You will save much time this way. (Note: Subscription services have more indexes than do free services.)

- You should take detailed notes as you go. Jot down contextual information and target information. List names of people, committees, subcommittees, and bill or law citations mentioned in the target record. Why? If your first search method fails, these notes can restart your search; they give you alternative ways to search.

You can use what you know to find what you want. For example, if a student intern researching elder healthcare jots down key terms, citations, names, and dates as she works in a database of government records, she is prepared to search by any of these alternatives:

- By subjects discussed in the record (for example, elder health care)
- By citation (number and letter "addresses") of a particular legislative record in a system of citation, (for example, H.R. 1091–106 for a particular House of Representatives bill)
- By names, dates, committees, or other elements of a legislative process (for example, the name of the senator sponsoring a bill)

In other words, she could find legislation on elder healthcare by subject (elder healthcare, nursing home care, Medicare, and so on), or by citation (H.R. 1091–106), or by legislative process information (Senator Ted Kennedy; hearing witness Donna Shalala, Department of Health and Human Services; Senate Committee on Health, Education, Labor, and Pensions).

Task # 3. Write the legislative history document

To write your legislative history, begin by using the Method in chapter 2. You can reuse the thinking that went into planning your research (see *Strategy* in How to, this chapter). Use it to plan your legislative history document. Let your intended reader's needs for the information guide your selection of information for the history.

What is the message of a legislative history? It is your conclusion formed after consulting the record. The history's scope is set by the purpose (whether you are writing a law history or an issue history) and by the amount of information required to support your message. In any case, you must organize your information to support the message. Organizational options include chronology (to show developments over time), significance (to highlight influential legislation), and trend (to show a pattern).

If no form is prescribed for presenting the results of your research, you might choose to use the following standard reporting format for professional and technical communication:

- Overview that concisely summarizes both the message and the key information in the document
- Subsections that provide summaries of information
- Subheadings that label each subsection
- Citations that are provided for each subsection

Citation is very important in a legislative history. The history's credibility and the practical needs of the information user (and the researcher) demand that all sources be easy to locate for confirmation and referral. Citations are the means of doing so. A full citation provides three kinds of information about a source: what type of record it is, how it is classified in a system of documentation, who publishes it (a commercial research service or government). For government records, a full citation includes all the elements that help to identify a source. In legislative research, a full citation, or government style, is preferred over a terse citation, or legal style, that provides only an abbreviated source identifier, number in a system of documentation, and date. If either the government style or legal style is prescribed for you, use that style. If not, choose the appropriate style and use it exclusively. Do not mix styles.

Here is a list of the elements in a full citation, or government style, for citing federal or state legislation:

- Issuing agency (house, number, session, year)
- Title (document number and name; long name may be abbreviated)
- Edition or version
- Imprint (city, publisher, date of publication)
- Series (serial list of publications)
- Notes (in parentheses, add anything not already included in the citation that helps to locate the document)

Following are two illustrations of government style:

1. U.S. House. 101st Congress, 1st Session (1989). H.R. 1946, A Bill to...Authorize the Department of Veterans Affairs (VA) to Provide Home, Respite, and Dental Care. Washington: Government Printing Office, 1990. (GPO Microfiche no. 393, coordinate C13.)

2. U.S. House. 104th Congress, 1st Session (1995). "H.R. 3, A Bill to Control Crime." Version: 1; Version Date: 2/9/93. (Full Text of Bills: Congressional Universe Online Service. Bethesda, MD: Congressional Information Service.)

In the second illustration, the final element shows that the source is proprietary, or a commercial research service publication available to paying subscribers.

If you need more help on citing, see

- Diane L. Garner and Diane H. Smith, *The complete guide to citing government information resources: a manual for writers and librarians* (rev. ed.) (Bethesda, MD: Congressional Information Service, 1993)

- Citing Government Information Sources Using MLA (Modern Language Association) Style at http://www.knowledgecenter. unr.edu/subjects/guides/government/cite.html

- Uncle Sam: Brief Guide to Citing Government Publications (University of Memphis Depository Library) at http://exlibris. memphis.edu/resource/unclesam/citeweb.html

- How Do I? Cite Publications Found in Databases for Thomas (Library of Congress) at http://thomas.loc.gov/tfaqs/16.htm

Remember to check your final product against the standard (see checklists, chapter 2).

Three Examples

Example 1. The Legislative History of Nutritional Labeling 1906–1987

Overview

Government has debated the topic of food labeling for nearly 100 years. Its history of legislation passed and court cases settled shows where we've come from and sets a precedent for future legislation. In 1906 Congress was concerned with establishing a basic standard for product labels to prevent consumers from being misled. Since then changes in science and public opinion have necessitated drafting new bills that fill gaps in legislation and place more restrictions on product labels to better protect and inform consumers. In the late 1980's that meant requiring nutritional labels on pre-packaged grids listing calories, fat, sugars, and other food values to inform an increasingly health-conscious America. Now in 2002, America's growing taste for increased portions of unhealthy fast food must be addressed by filling the gap in the Nutritional Labeling and Education Act exempting fast food from nutritional labels.

Major Legislation and Legal Decisions
59th Congress

H.R. *384: "The Food and Drug Act of 1906."* This act was the first on record in the United States that governed the contents of product labels. The legislature was concerned that manufacturers and distributors were labeling their products in a manner that misled consumers. Product labels that falsified ingredients or other product information were considered "adulterated" by the act. Through this legislation, food and drugs were required to be labeled with "distinctive names" that pertained directly to their contents and to have those names and the manufacturers' locations printed clearly. To enforce this bill, the Department of Agriculture was empowered to inspect, on demand, all packaged goods manufactured or transported within the United States, levying fines on violators.

76th Congress

S.5: "The Federal Food, Drug and Cosmetic Act of 1938." This legislation was intended to replace the Food and Drug Act and cover a greater variety of products, including cosmetics, with more specific language that clarified vagueness in the 1906 act. The new act regulated items on store shelves (an important addition), broadened the definition of "adulterated" to include spoiled or mishandled food, and placed tighter restrictions on how food could be labeled. If products claimed to serve specific dietary needs or produce certain health benefits, their labels had to contain a list of ingredients and be approved by the Secretary of Agriculture. The Secretary could now freely inspect not only the goods themselves, but also any factory, warehouse, or establishment that produced, stored, or sold them and freeze the sale of products that could be considered "adulterated." This was deemed much more effective than fines in deterring violators.[2]

85th Congress

H.R. 13254: "Food Additives Amendment." Created to amend the Federal Food, Drug and Cosmetic Act to cover food additives. This amendment shows government recognition of a growing trend in the food industry to use food additives and flavor enhancers with possible adverse health effects in order to lower costs. This amendment requires that before any food additive or flavor enhancer is used, its producers must disclose the additive's chemical composition and the results of a certified health study attesting to the additive's safety in the specific dosage. The effect was a dramatic decrease in the use of sodium and its derivatives as preserving agents.[3]

95th Congress

S.1750: "Saccharin Study and Labeling Act of 1977." This legislation is an extension of the Food Additives Amendment that called for the study of a possible link between saccharin consumption and cancer. At time of passage, saccharin, a sugar substitute, was a tremendously popular product and the implication that its usage could cause cancer was serious. The study found a conclusive link between saccharin usage and increased incidence of cancer in laboratory animals but it could not convince legislators there was a significant risk to humans. Instead of upsetting the marketplace based on "inconclusive" results, the Health, Labor, Education, and Pensions Committee implemented mandatory labeling. All products containing saccharin must clearly state: "Use of this product may be hazardous to your health. This product contains saccharin which has been determined to cause cancer in laboratory animals." What makes this bill noteworthy is that legislators approved of allowing an ingredient with alleged health risks to remain on the market provided that it had a clearly stated health advisory on the packaging.[4]

96th Congress

S.1196: "Disease Prevention and Health Promotion Act of 1978." The applicability of this legislation is its position on the effectiveness of disease prevention programs. The Committee on Health, Labor, Education, and Pensions found that contrary to popular opinion, "Americans are not fully informed about how to improve their own health and want more knowledge, that Federal, State and local governments have a role to play in providing that information, and that government at all levels has the capacity and the responsibility to help communities and individuals reduce the burden of illness through the prevention of disease and the promotion of good health."[5]

99th Congress

S.541: "Nutrition Information Labeling Act of 1985." A bill to amend the Federal Food, Drug and Cosmetic Act to require that a food's product label state the specific, common-name and the amount of each fat or oil contained in the food, the amount of saturated, polyunsaturated, and monounsaturated fats contained in the food, the amount of cholesterol contained in the food, and the amount of sodium and potassium contained in the food. This is the first bill to require nutritional labels, although it does not cover restaurants or raw agricultural products.[6]

99th Congress

H.R. 6940: "Amend Food, Drug and Cosmetic Act." This bill requires baby formula to contain a prescribed nutritional content in order to be sold in the US. The significance is that government recognizes the need to not only disclose nutritional content but also regulate that content in order to ensure the well-being of the consumer.[7]

Arbitration

In response to two petitions filed by The Center for Science in the Public Interest, New York State filed suit against McDonalds Corp. alleging that their Chicken McNuggets were not the "pure chicken" advertised. In an out-of-court settlement McDonalds Corp. agreed to withdraw the ads and disclose the ingredients and nutritional content of their menu in pamphlets and posters at their New York restaurants. At the same time attorneys general in ten other states began the process of filing suit to require nutritional and ingredient disclosures from McDonalds and other major fast food chains. In a national settlement still in effect, McDonalds, Burger King, Jack in the Box, Kentucky Fried Chicken, and Wendy's agreed to offer separately printed nutritional information in pamphlets or on posters in stores around the country. This action resulted in McDonalds cutting back on beef-frying and discontinuing the use of yellow dye No. 5, which has been known to trigger allergies. However long-term compliance with the settlement has been inconsistent and only Jack in the Box has made information consistently available nationally. The rest of the chains only provided them in an average of 33 percent of locations.[8,9]

100th Congress

S.1325: "Fast Food Ingredient Information Act of 1987." This bill was written in response to a greater nutritional consciousness and the national settlement mentioned in the lawsuit above. The bill sought to amend the Food, Drug and Cosmetic Act to force fast food restaurants to label pre-packaged goods with nutritional labels and to display nutritional and ingredient information in clearly visible places in their restaurants. The bill also sought to amend the Federal Meat Inspection Act and the Poultry Products Inspection Act to allow for nutritional information to be posted in restaurants. President Reagan vetoed this bill because of possible, negative economic consequences.[10]

101st Congress

H.R. 3562: "The Nutrition Labeling and Education Act of 1989." An amendment to the Food, Drug and Cosmetic Act designed to expand on the requirements of the Nutritional Labeling and Education Act. The bill states that food will be deemed misbranded unless its label contains: serving size, number of servings, calories per serving and those derived from fat and saturated fat, and the amount of choles-terol, sodium, total carbohydrates, sugars, total protein, and dietary fiber per serving or other unit. Authorizes the Secretary of Health and Human Services to require additional label information.[11]

Sources

1. U.S. House of Representatives. 59th Congress. 2nd Session (1906). "H.R. 384 Food and Drug Act of 1906." Washington Government Printing Office, 1981.
2. U.S. Senate. 76th Congress. 1st Session (1938). "S.5 Federal Food, Drug and Cosmetic Act of 1938." Washington Government Printing Office, 1981.
3. U.S. House of Representatives. 85th Congress. 2nd Session (1958). "H.R. 13254 Food Additives Amendment." Washington Government Printing Office, 1981.
4. U.S. Senate. 95th Congress. 2nd Session (1977). "S.1750 Saccharin Study and Labeling Act of 1977." Washington Government Printing Office, 1978 (Thomas Bill Summary S.1750).
5. U.S. Senate. 96th Congress. 1st Session (1978). "S.1196 Disease Prevention and Health Promotion Act of 1978." Washington Government Printing Office, 1980 (Thomas Bill Summary S.1196).
6. U.S. Senate. 99th Congress. 1st Session (1985). "S.541 Nutrition Information Labeling Act of 1985." Washington Government Printing Office, 1985 (Thomas Bill Summary S.541).
7. U.S. House of Representatives. 99th Congress. 2nd Session (1986). "H.R. 6940 Amend Food, Drug and Cosmetic Act." Washington Government Printing Office, 1986 (Thomas Bill Summary H.R. 6940).
8. Clark, Charles S. "The Fast Food Shake-Up." *CQ Researcher,* November 8, 1991: 838–43.

9. *McDonalds to Introduce Nutrition Information Programs in New York: Press Release.* 30 April 1986. New York: New York State Attorney General's Office Consumer Protection Bureau.

10. U.S. Senate. 100th Congress. 1st Session (1987). "S.1325 Fast Food Ingredient Information Act of 1987." Washington Government Printing Office, 1987 (Thomas Bill Summary S.1325).

11. U.S. House of Representatives. 101st Congress. 1st Session (1989). "H.R. 3562 The Nutrition Labeling and Education Act of 1989." Washington Government Printing Office, 1989 (Thomas Bill Summary H.R. 3562).

What this example shows. This history of an issue includes litigation as well as multiple, selected legislative actions (*Scope*, this chapter). The author chose a report as the medium or presentation. It is titled, as a report typically is, rather than provided with a header, as a memo typically is. The title and overview connect this report to a context, a process underway in 2002 to amend existing legislation proposed in 1989. This report traces landmark legislation leading up to the 1989 bill, the most recent action on the subject.

Organizationally, the report begins with an initial overview followed by summaries of major legislation arranged chronologically. Subheadings (congressional session and date) move an unfolding story of action along. Each summary concludes with a statement of the act's significance in a trend. The message of the report is to show that trend (Method, chapter 2). Thus, the concluding sentence of each summary reinforces the message by adding a new bit to the reader's recognition of the trend.

No purpose or audience for this report is identified; the undergraduate policy writing course assignment that prompted the research did not require it. That is a limitation on real world use, but this document nonetheless meets some of the expected standards for usability. It could serve a nonprofit organization wishing to inform its members about a current legislative priority.

Credibility is enhanced by the report's organization, which suggests care taken by an informed author to select key actions (well cited). Presentation here is authoritative and readable. The author has recognized a legislative trend and has selected, condensed, and ordered relevant legislation as well as litigation to highlight milestones in that trend. These choices and communication techniques encourage readers to agree with his position that new action is needed.

Careful citation here supports credibility. Readability is served by the way citations are handled. Citations are distributed across two locations in the text. Subheadings for summaries cite the legislative session, record number, and common name of each bill; a footnote at the end of each summary refers to citations at the end of the document, where the act is fully referenced using government record identifiers and bibliographic style (Task #3, this chapter, and checklists, chapter 2).

The document is designed for use. Despite its brevity, it could be more concise. Sentences are typically long and many sentences include unnecessary words (checklists, chapter 2). The writer could shorten sentences to emphasize key information better, as illustrated below.

Original. The bill sought to amend the Food, Drug and Cosmetic Act to force fast food restaurants to label pre-packaged goods with nutritional labels and to display nutritional and ingredient information in clearly visible places in their restaurants. The bill also sought to amend the Federal Meat Inspection Act and the Poultry Products Inspection Act to allow for nutritional information to be posted in restaurants. (65 words)

Revised. The bill amends the Food, Drug and Cosmetic Act to require nutritional labeling of pre-packaged goods and clearly visible display of ingredients by fast food restaurants. The Federal Meat Inspection Act and the Poultry Products Inspection Act are amended to allow ingredients display in restaurants. (45 words; 20 word reduction or 30% briefer)

The revision removes repetition of words ("bill sought to amend" and "nutritional information") and unnecessary explanation ("in clearly visible places").

Example 2. The Legislative History of Banning the Use of Cell Phones While Driving

Memorandum

To: North Carolina General Assembly Senator Dannelly; Representatives McAllister, Adams, B., Allen, Harrell, Hunter, Jones, Luebke, Michaux, Parmon, Tolson, and Womble.

From: AARP Steering Committee (simulated)

Date: April 7, 2008

Re: Ban on Cell Phones While Driving: A Legislative History

Overview

Driver distractions lead each year to thousands of unnecessary and preventable deaths on our nation's streets and highways. One such distraction is the use of cell phones while driving. In his article analyzing legislative attempts to regulate cell phone use, Matthew Kalin cites studies that estimate "that six-hundred thousand collisions occur each year because of cellular phone use in vehicles" and that "ten to one-thousand deaths per year" occur as a result of cell phone use in vehicles (Kalin, 262, n 21). Other researchers have compared people talking on a cell phone while driving to drunk drivers. In a 2006 study of drivers in a driving simulator, professors at the University of Utah found that "people are as impaired when they drive and talk on a cell phone as they are when they drive intoxicated at the legal blood-alcohol limit of 0.08 percent" (Strayer, Drews & Crouch, 385–90). Lives can easily be saved by banning the use of cell phones while driving.

The North Carolina legislature has made a good start in this area. Current legislation protects our children from bus drivers distracted by their cell phones (N.C.G.S. §20-140.6) and inexperienced drivers are not allowed to use a cell phone while driving (N.C.G.S. §20-137.3). Unfortunately, your bills to amend Chapter 20 of the North Carolina General Statutes to ban the use of cell phones by all drivers have not yet been passed into law.

The following review of current legislation shows that the important work of making our streets and highways safer from the dangers posed by distracted drivers has begun. Unfortunately, current legislation falls dangerously short in the area of cell phone use by drivers. For now, current legislation only forbids a fraction of the millions of people driving while using their cell phones. Consequently, we can expect innocent motorists and pedestrians to continue to be injured and killed on our roads and highways by drivers too caught up with their telephone conversations to pay attention to their surroundings. Now is the time to resume your call to protect everyone on our roads and highways from the danger posed by drivers distracted by cell phone use. North Carolina can become a leader in protecting motorists from the deadly consequences of drivers distracted by their cell phones by banning the use of cell phones by all drivers.

Major Legislation–North Carolina

General Assembly of North Carolina, 2005 Session

Senate Bill 1289 (Third Edition): "Cell Phone Use by Drivers Under 18 Prohibited" (G.S. 20-137.3). This Bill makes it illegal for drivers between the ages of 15 and 18 years of age to use a cell phone while driving. Specifically, this bill

- Makes the use of a cell phone by a person between the ages of 15 and 18 years of age while driving an infraction
- Provides for a fine of $25 (but does not assess court costs or result in points against the driver's license or insurance)
- Further punishes a teenage driver by not allowing the driver to advance to the next level of licensure for an additional 6 months
- Includes a ban on the use of hands-free phones, Internet gaming devices, electronic music devices, and the like.

General Assembly of North Carolina, 2007 Session

House Bill 183 (Third Edition): "Ban Cell Phone Use by School Bus Drivers" (G.S. 20-140.6). This Bill created Section 20-140.6 of the North Carolina General Statutes, making it illegal to "engage in a call on a mobile phone or use a digital media device while operating a public or private school bus" (N.C.G.S. §20-140.6). Specifically, this bill

- Makes the use of a cell phone by a bus driver a Class 2 misdemeanor
- Provides for a punishment of up to 60 days and a fine of no less than $100
- Allows for emergency exceptions

While the above protections are an important start, the AARP agrees with you that more is required. We applaud the following two bills that all of you worked so diligently on and hope you will continue your good work and see them passed into law. In fact, we encourage you to go even further in the name of safety—consider banning all cell telephone use (with the current exceptions), *including* hands-free phones.

Senate Bill 1399: "Ban Mobile Phone Use While Driving." This bill was re-referred to the Committee on Judiciary II (Criminal) on May 24, 2007. If passed, it would ban the use of cell phones while driving, but allow drivers to use hands-free phones while driving. It also allows for emergency exceptions and use by police, firefighters, and ambulance drivers. The use of a cell phone would be an infraction, with a penalty of a fine of $25.00. There would be no point assessment to the driver's North Carolina driver's license nor any insurance surcharge assessed as a result of a violation of this section. Also, this infraction would "not constitute negligence per se or contributory negligence by the driver in any action for the recovery of damages arising out of the operation, ownership, or maintenance of a motor vehicle."

House Bill 1104: "Ban Cell Phone Use While Driving." This bill was re-referred to the Committee on Judiciary III on May 18, 2005. If passed, it would ban the use of cell phones while driving, but allow drivers to use hands-free phones while driving. It also allows for emergency exceptions and use by police, firefighters, and ambulance drivers. The use of a cell phone while driving would be an infraction, with a penalty of a $100.00 fine and costs of court. No points would be assessed to the driver's North Carolina driver's license as a result of this infraction.

Legislation in Other Jurisdictions

According to a 2004 review of traffic safety legislation, eighteen states and the District of Columbia have passed laws regarding the use of cell phones while driving (Savage, Sundeen and Mejeur, 2004). Below is a sample of the legislation currently in effect in other states:

California: Section 23103 of the California Vehicle Code makes it illegal to operate a handheld device while driving, and the fine is $20.00 for the first offense and $50.00 for each offense thereafter (Barmby, 345).

New York: Section 1225 of the New York code bans the use of hand-held cell phones while driving, and a violation of same is considered an infraction, punishable by a fine of not more than $100.00 (New York Consolidated Law Service).

New Jersey: Section 39:4-97.3 of the New Jersey Statutes makes it illegal to use a cell phone while driving unless it is a "hands-free wireless telephone." A driver in New Jersey can be cited for such a violation only if she is detained for another driving or criminal violation at the same time. A person who violates this law is to be fined "no less than

$100 or more than $250" and no points are assessed to the driver's license or insurance (LexisNexis New Jersey Annotated Statutes).

In addition to state legislation, a number of towns and cities implemented their own bans on the use of cell phones while driving. Brooklyn, Ohio was the first municipality in the U.S. to ban cellular phone use while driving, and Hilltown, Pennsylvania, also banned the use of cell phones while driving (Kalin, 244). Fort Campbell military base in Kentucky banned hand-held cellular phone use while driving (Kalin, 245). However, as you know, municipality ordinances can be overruled by a state law, "preemption," if the state legislators think it appropriate.

Again, we hope North Carolina can become a leader in providing for safer streets and highways by banning both hand-held *and hands-free* cell phone use while driving.

Federal Response

On July 18, 2000, Congress began hearings to discuss possible legislative solutions (Cripps, 107). The House of Representatives introduced the Driver Distraction Prevention Act of 2000, a study implemented to explore the impact of driver distractions on highway safety (Cripps, 107). However, to date, Congress has not implemented a policy to protect drivers from the hazards posed by drivers distracted by cell phone use.

Works Cited

Barmby, Erin. "Review of selected 2007 California legislation: Vehicle: Chapter 290: California's message to hang up and pay attention." McGeorge Law Review 38 (2007): 42–52.

Cripps, Jr., Jesse. "Dialing while driving: The battle over cell phone use on America's roadways." Gonzaga Law Review 37 (2001/2002): 89–119.

House Bill 183. "Ban cell phone use while driving." Online: North Carolina General Assembly homepage 9 April 2008. http://www.ncleg.net/gascripts/BillLookUp/BillLookUp.pl?Session=2005&BillID=H1104

Kalin, Matthew. "The 411 on cellular phone use: An analysis of the legislative attempts to regulate cellular phone use by drivers." Suffolk University Law Review 39 (January 2005): 233–262. Citing, Hahn, Robert & Patrick M. Dudley. "The disconnect between law and policy analysis: A case study of drivers and cell phones, Administrative Law Review 55 (2003): 127, 130.

New Jersey Statutes Annotated 39:4–97.3 (2004). Online: LexisNexis (TM) New Jersey Annotated Statutes 8 April 2008. http://www.lexisnexis.com/us [Subscription required] New York Vehicle & Traffic Law 1225-c (2001). Online: New York Consolidated Law Service, Matthew Bender & Company, Inc. 8 April 2008. http://www.lexisnexis.com/us/ [Subscription required]

Savage, Melissa, Sundeen, Matt, and Mejeur, Jeanne, "Traffic safety and public health: State legislative Action, 2004." National Conference of State Legislators' Transportation Series, (December 2004, No. 20). Online, 8 April 2008. http://www.ncsl.org/print/transportation/04trafficsafety.pdf

Senate Bill 1399. "Ban mobile phone use while driving." Online: North Carolina General Assembly homepage. 9 April 2008. http://www.ncleg.net/gascripts/BillLookUp/BillLookUp.pl?BillID=S1399&Session=2007

Strayer, David, Frank Drews & Dennis Crouch. "A comparison of the cell phone driver and the drunk driver." Human Factors 48 (Summer 2006): 381–391.

Stutts, Jane, Donald Reinfurt, Loren Staplin & Eric Rodgman. "The role of driver distraction in traffic crashes." AAA Foundation for Traffic Safety Report. (May 2001): 1–63. Online: 9 April 2008. http://www.aaafoundation.org/pdf/distraction.pdf

---

Example 3. The Legislative History of the Criminalization of Cocaine

Memorandum

To: Legislative Committee Members

From: Citizens Against Racial Enforcement of Drug Laws, "C.A.R.E." (simulated)

Date: February 18, 2008

Re: Realignment of the Criminalization of Illicit Drugs To Treatment: Advocacy with Supporting Legislative History

Overview

The non-medical use of cocaine was federally regulated for the first time in 1914 with the passage of the Harrison Act in 1914 ("Drug Facts"). Since then, the government has devoted considerable efforts and resources to the fight against illicit drugs in our country. In fact, this policy area is most commonly referred to in terms of violent metaphors, including, for example, the "war on drugs." Because we are in a "war against drugs," our policy response focuses not on helping people with drug addiction problems (although drug prevention and treatment are a part of the policy response), but on "defeating our enemy." However, our "enemy" in this war is our own citizens who have become addicted to drugs. While the legislation summarized below often refers to treatment efforts, only a very small percentage of resources are actually devoted to treatment. According to Jim Moye, an attorney with the District of Columbia Office of Corporation Counsel, "only four cents of every dollar budgeted is spent on drug prevention and treatment" (Moye, 276).

Another aspect of the criminalization of drugs is that it leaves the production and distribution in the hands of criminals. This system, then, creates a criminal underclass to fill the need for drugs. This illegal system is ruled by violence and there is little to no concern for the safety of the actual product (either in terms of appropriate dosing or in materials used to create or to "cut" the pure drug).

Finally, there are significant costs associated with the war on drugs. First, there are significant resources devoted to the arrest, prosecution and imprisonment of people who use illicit drugs. Vast sums of resources are spent each year by law enforcement, the court system, and the prison system on this war on drugs. One estimate places the U.S. government spending approximately $26 billion a year on the war on drugs (Moye, 276). A second significant cost consideration is the loss of potential tax revenues from the sale of drugs. A final significant cost in the war on drugs is the loss of respect for the legal system by certain citizens. Studies show the current policy appears to disproportionately impact African-Americans. For example, University of Chicago Law School Professor Tracey L. Meares cites a study that provides that "in 1993, African Americans comprised 35% of those arrested for drug offenses, 55% of those convicted for drug offenses, and 74% of those who received prison sentences for drug offenses" (Meares, 140).

While there is a large number of drugs that are illegal to possess, manufacture, distribute, and so on, we address only cocaine as a starting point for the possible transition from a focus on punishment to a focus on treatment for drug abusers in our country. If cocaine were legalized, then the resources currently devoted to enforcing and imprisoning cocaine users could be diverted to drug prevention and treatment programs. Also, and importantly, the government would no longer have to define a portion of its constituents as an "enemy."

The legislative summaries that follow describe a federal response to our drug problem that ostensibly provides for both law enforcement and treatment. Unfortunately, the reality is that this legislation results in a system where nearly all of the available resources are devoted to law enforcement and punishment, not treatment.

Major Legislation
91st Congress
H.R. 18583: "Comprehensive Drug Abuse Prevention and Control Act of 1970." This Act was designed to increase research into and prevention of "drug abuse and drug dependence," provide for "treatment and rehabilitation of drug abusers," and to "strengthen existing

law enforcement authority" in the area of drug abuse. This Act became Public Law No. 91-513 on October 27, 1970.

This Act was promulgated before the introduction of "crack cocaine." Crack cocaine became a cheap alternative to other illicit drugs and resulted in what many referred to as an epidemic.

99th Congress

H.R. 5484: "Anti-Drug Abuse Act of 1986." This Act was designed to "strengthen Federal efforts" to halt "international drug traffic…provide strong Federal leadership in establishing effective drug abuse prevention and…to…support drug abuse treatment and rehabilitation efforts." Among other things, this Act increased criminal penalties for drug trafficking, permits the seizure and forfeiture of property or funds involved in money laundering, provides grants to states for treatment, prevention and rehabilitation programs, and shares the sense of Congress that the media should refrain from "producing material that glamorizes" illegal drugs.

Other than block grants to the states for treatment efforts, this Act focuses on reinforcing the federal government's ability to fight illicit drugs by increasing the punishment levels for trafficking and by expanding the scope of the criminal arm of the law to include the seizure and forfeiture of property or funds in the hands of "money launderers." The focus of this Act is made clear by the power the federal government kept—the ability to fight against illegal drugs. Treatment efforts, on the other hand, are passed on to the states as block grants. Treatment efforts, then, became as varied as the states themselves, with no central or powerful voice in government.

100th Congress

H.R. 5210: "Anti-Drug Abuse Act of 1988." This Act is designed to "prevent the manufacturing, distribution, and use of illicit drugs." Among other things, this Act increases the federal response to illicit drugs by establishing the Office of National Drug Control Policy and the position of the "drug czar," funds U.S. Attorneys and their staff for the purposes of pursuing asset forfeiture and other civil remedies, criminalizes trafficking in anabolic steroids and prohibits the sale of certain consumer products containing butyl nitrite ("poppers"), establishes the "sense of Congress in opposition to the legalization of illegal drugs" by, among other things, making drug-related criminal activity grounds for termination of public housing tenancies and declaring the policy that America would be "drug-free" by 1995, and establishes the death penalty for certain Federal drug-related crimes. As with the

Anti-Drug Abuse Act of 1986, the treatment provisions are limited to block grants—it amends the Public Health Service Act to provide for block grants to states for alcohol, drug abuse, and mental illness prevention and treatment, and research.

Again, this legislation evinces a clear focus by the federal government on law enforcement, with the treatment components being limited to a block grant system.

Relevant Legal Opinions

While there are myriad cases dealing with the issue of drug laws, one Supreme Court opinion reflects the phenomenon that occurs when our government is engaged in a "war"—a willingness to accept injury to innocent noncombatants. While injury to innocent people often happens in war (despite the best, and often heroic, efforts by military personnel to avoid it), our government should not be engaged in a war against its own citizens simply because those citizens have made the unhealthy choice to use illicit drugs. Our government should be treating their addiction, not waging war against them.

In the following decision, the U.S. Supreme Court ruled on the side of the drug enforcement community and allowed four poor, elderly citizens—all four of whom were innocent bystanders—to be evicted from their own homes.

Department of Housing and Urban Development v. Rucker, 535 U.S. 125 (2002): A provision in an amendment to the United States Housing Act of 1937 (this Act gave Congress the power to authorize public housing authorities) gives public housing authorities the right to punish people engaged in drug-related criminal activity. In *Rucker*, the U.S. Supreme Court found in favor of a public housing authority who evicted four so-called "innocent tenants" for the drug-related activities of their grandchildren, caregivers, and guests. The four defendants in this case were elderly long-time residents of public housing who were evicted by the Oakland Housing Authority, not for engaging in any kind of drug-related activity themselves, but for having family members or guests involved in drug activity on or simply near the Housing Authority premises.

Works Cited

1. Dep't of Housing & Urban Dev. v. Rucker, 535 U.S. 125 (2002).
2. Office of National Drug Control Policy. "Drug facts." Online: Lexis-Nexis 25 February 2008. http://www.whitehousedrugpolicy.gov/drugfact/cocaine/.
3. Mears, Tracey. "Symposium: Rethinking Federal criminal law: Charting race and class differences in attitudes toward drug legalization and law

enforcement: Lessons for Federal criminal law." Buffalo Criminal Law Review 1 (1997): 137–174.

4. Moye, Jim. "Can't stop the hustle: The Department of Housing and Urban Development's 'one strike' eviction policy fails to get drugs out of America's projects." Boston College Third World Law Journal 23 (2003): 275–292.

5. U.S. House, 91st Congress, 2nd Session (1970), H.R. 18583: Comprehensive Drug Abuse Prevention and Control Act of 1970. Online: Lexis-Nexis 25 February 2008. http://web.lexis-nexis.com/congcomp [Subscription required.]

6. U.S. House. 99th Congress, 1st Session (1986), H.R. 5484: Anti-Drug Abuse Act of 1986. Online: Thomas.loc.gov. 10 February 2008. http://thomas.loc.gov/cgibin/bdquery/z?d099:HR05484:@@@S. Public Law (P.L.)99–570. http://thomas.loc.gov/cgi-bin/bdquery/L?d099:./list/bd/d099pl.lst:501 [1–663](Public_Laws)|TOM:/bss/d099query.html|

7. U.S. 7. U.S. House. 100th Congress, 1st Session (1988), H.R. 5210: Anti-Drug Abuse Act of 1988. Online: Thomas.loc.gov. 10 February 2008. http://thomas.loc.gov/cgi-bin/bdquery/z?d100:HR05210:%7CTOM:/bss/d100query.html%7C.

***

What these examples show. These examples illustrate purposeful research for inquiry and reporting for advocacy. In both cases, the inquiring writer searched government records to inform the nonprofit organization's spokesperson (simulated) in preparation for requesting legislative action to regulate cell phone use (Example 2) or stating a position opposing the current direction of drug abuse policy (Example 3). Results of the records search are summarized in memos representing the organization and addressed to elected state-level officials (Example 2) and to unnamed federal-level committee members (Example 3).

In policy process terms, these documents typify the two main reasons for writing legislative histories, either to chronicle prior action (Example 2) or to characterize a pattern of legislative intent (Example 3).

They illustrate the typical actors in roles who generate and use information in a policy process. In both examples, nonprofit organizations (simulated) collect information for the purpose of persuading elected officials to solve a defined problem. If policy makers agree to take up the problem described in Example 2, makers of goods and providers of services in automobile, telephonic, and computer industries will likely join the debate, as will consumer organizations. Professionals outside government such as attorneys and legal services providers, public health care providers, lobbyists, and community advocates along with professional staff members inside government will likely be involved if the policy redirection advocated in Example 3 gains traction, as journalists like to say.

Intergovernmental action is illustrated in Example 2, where municipal, state, and federal responses are described.

Communication would be improved by reducing wordiness in both documents. Here is an illustration from Example 2.

Original. Unfortunately, your bills to amend Chapter 20 of the North Carolina General Statutes to ban the use of cell phones by all drivers have not yet been passed into law.

The following review of current legislation shows that the important work of making our streets and highways safer from dangers posed by distracted drivers has begun. Unfortunately, current legislation falls dangerously short in the area of cell phone use by drivers. (72 words)

Revised. Unfortunately, your amendments to Chapter 20 to ban the use of cell phones by all drivers are not yet law.

The following review of current legislation shows that the important work of making our streets and highways safer has begun. But it falls short of banning all drivers' use of cell phones. (50 words)

The revision removes repetition ("dangers," "dangerously," "unfortunately," "current legislation") and excess procedural detail ("have not been passed into law"). It retains other repetition needed for accuracy in context ("use of cell phones by all drivers").

Summary and Preview

To persuasively ask for government action, you must know what government has done, has not done, or has intended in regard to your concern. Legislative records research informs you. Legislative history reporting enables you to inform others. This chapter prepares you to do both. Chapter 5, next, prepares you to use your knowledge of the record to make your argument.

Position Paper: Know the Arguments

Key Concept

- Policy argumentation

Making public policy requires making arguments and understanding arguments. This chapter helps you to argue a position, to critically analyze your own and other arguments, and to recognize grounds for cooperation as well as competition among arguments.

A policy argument supports a claim that something should or should not be done. Such arguments have two main components: a claim and its support. The claim asserts what should or should not be done. Or it takes a position on a debated question. Support for the claim presents the facts, interpretations, and assumptions that lead to making that claim. The argument's presentation should be intentionally constructed to convince others to accept the claim and to agree with the position.

Arguments are made both implicitly and explicitly. Implicit arguments are unstated elements of problem definitions. For example, to define cell phone use while driving as a public safety risk is to argue implicitly that government has a role in regulating drivers' risky behaviors. Implicit arguments are usually not intended to deceive. They are simply the unacknowledged structures of thought within a position. Position takers should be critically aware of their implicit arguments and their explicit arguments. They should critically analyze other positions for implicit arguments, as well.

Why argue? In policy work, you argue to disclose what you think and what you want to accomplish. You do not argue to prove or disprove; you do not argue only for or against. The popular notion of argument as a quarrel between adversaries distorts argument's function and significance for policy purposes. Similarly, the legal notion of argument as contestation by opposing parties is inadequate. In policy making, there are always more than two interested parties. In democratic process, you engage ideas, not adversaries. You argue to add your position to the debate and to the possibilities.

To illustrate, an undergraduate student government representative wants to change the culture at her university to discourage drug and alcohol abuse. As a dormitory resident advisor, she knows first hand that campus culture encourages recreational drug use and underage as well as binge drinking. Initially, she took the position that punitive action was called for. As a member of the Judicial Affairs subcommittee of the student assembly, she had accomplished revisions in the university judicial system to increase sanctions against drug and alcohol use as well as penalties for violations. However, the sanctions and penalties had little impact on the character of campus life. Consequently, her position has changed. In a report that she authors for the student assembly's Judicial Affairs subcommittee addressed to the Dean of Student Affairs, she now argues that judicial action is not enough. She cites evidence from dormitory life based on her resident advising experience. She claims that comprehensive action is needed to reduce dependence on drugs and alcohol for social interaction. She specifies needs to update university policy, to reorganize administration of campus life, and to design educational interventions. In her choice of proposed solutions, she has anticipated opposing arguments by other student government leaders and by some university administrators favoring either the status quo or increased sanctions and enforcement. Her purpose for arguing is to deepen the campus debate on drugs and alcohol by focusing on the central question of why campus life encourages their use.

At the same university, another undergraduate majoring in public policy studies serves as an officer of a national student association that advocates drug policy reform. In that role, she writes a policy memo to the director of a national drug control policy institute stating her association's position on recent legislation and asking the director to rethink the institute's support for recent amendments to the Higher Education Act (HEA) of 1965. (Proposals to amend typically refer to the original legislation being amended. Major acts such as the 1965 HEA are amended often over many years.) Those amendments barred students with drug-related convictions from receiving federal financial aid for education unless they undergo rehabilitation. The student leader presents the association's opposition to the amendments on two grounds, fairness and feasibility. On fairness, she argues that reducing eligibility for aid to higher education hurts working class families and discriminates against people of color. Regarding the discriminatory effects, she elaborates with empirical evidence showing that 95% of imprisoned drug offenders in New York State are people of color while the majority of drug users are not. She interprets this evidence as showing racial bias in drug law enforcement at the state level. On feasibility, she argues that the amendments cannot be implemented because they do not call for allocation of funds to pay for rehabilitation. She anticipates rebuttals by the director of the drug control policy institute but she does not respond to them in the policy memo. Its purpose is to represent the student association's perspective on a current drug policy reform proposal.

What does policy argument do? It displays the reasoning that underlies positions. In collective public deliberation, arguments disclose the universe of definitions of the problem. In practical politics, argument reveals commonalities and conflicts. These are the grounds on which a course of action can be deliberated. Commonalities among arguments can point to potential cooperation, perhaps compromise, cosponsorship, or coalition forming. Conflicts give insight into competing interests and values that must be taken into account in negotiating a solution.

In another illustration, a farmer has applied to local government for a permit to operate a large-scale industrial farm called a confined animal feeding operation (CAFO). In the rural municipality where the farmer lives, the zoning ordinance allows such operations only as a "conditional" use of land zoned for agricultural uses. "Conditional" uses require case-by-case decisions by local officials on whether to permit or not permit the use. The decision process includes a public hearing inviting residents and others to comment on the proposed use. In the hearing held on the farmer's application, arguments including the following are made:

- Farmers have rights to use and to benefit from their property; to deny this permit is to violate the farmer's private property rights.

- Nearby home owners have rights to use and to benefit from their property; to grant this permit is to violate the neighbors' private property rights.

- Large-scale confined animal farming pollutes the environment and creates human health risks; to grant this permit is to fail to protect natural resources and the public welfare.

- Large-scale confined animal farming is regulated and better monitored for compliance with antipollution control than unregulated small-scale farming; to grant this permit will not harm local water or community health.

- Farming is an endangered occupation; to grant this permit will enable a local family-owned farm to succeed by expanding operations and will help to preserve farming in the region.

- Farming is an endangered occupation, and industrial farming is driving smaller farmers out of business; to grant this permit is to harm the local economy, which is still based on diverse types of farming.

If you were a local official, how would you decide this request? Clearly, many arguable issues and competing positions are involved. You might permit or not permit the use, basing your decision either way on a single argument. Alternatively, you might focus on a commonality among the arguments, such as the wish to preserve rights or the wish to protect public health. Then you might ask the farmer and the neighbors to work out a compromise application. You might delay your decision until you have a revised application that takes specified risks to the community into account.

Argument has its limits in practical policy work, of course. "Arguments are made by all players all the time; as a result they have limited effectiveness. Although arguments are a necessary ingredient to any strategy, they never work by themselves" (Coplin and O'Leary 1998). As the local government illustration suggests, you might need to craft a political compromise along with arguing your position. Also, you must recognize political conditions that will determine your argument's effectiveness. How well an argument is received has more to do with majority control in a governing body than with the quality of the argument. In the local government illustration, the official who represents majority political power might have sufficient influence to force a compromise. The minority power representative might not, unless others can be persuaded to join the minority's position.

When is argument important? Argument can make a difference at several points in the process. Arguments matter before a policy process begins, as positions are being developed. They matter at the outset of a process, as stakes are declared and agendas set. They matter again at the end of the process, when a decision is being made.

How to Argue in a Position Paper

Goal: Critical awareness of your own position, critical understanding of other positions, and willingness to consider and to engage other positions.

Objective: Reasoned argument for a position showing awareness of alternative positions and reasoning.

Product: Written document that explicitly argues and aims to persuade. A genre commonly used by policy analysts outside government is the position paper (sometimes called a discussion paper or "white" paper). Products might run to book-length in some circumstances, or they might be much shorter, perhaps two to six pages.

Scope: Either a "big picture" of conditions, causes, or consequences relating to a problem or a "little picture" of significant particulars.

Strategy: To know your position in relation to others. To consider your position ethically and politically

- make a list of the known positions on the problem;
- ask and answer the questions "What does my position have in common with others on this list?" and "How does my position differ from or conflict with others on the list?";
- note specific commonalities, differences, and conflicts of values, assumptions, or ideas between your position and other positions;
- identify potential grounds for cooperation and for competition.

Task #1. Outline your argument

If you are authoring a position paper for a professional association or for a nonprofit organization, make sure you understand its mission and how the position you are taking relates to the mission. Be clear on that relationship. Consult before deviating from the mission.

In most cases, you can use the following outline for informal arguments to construct the logic of a policy position:

- Problem
- Issue
- Question about the issue that has at least two answers and is therefore arguable
- Claim (the arguer's assertion or answer to the question)
- Support:
  - Justification
    1. Reasons ("because" or the relevance of the assertion)
    2. Assumptions ("basis" or the values, beliefs, principles, and licenses that motivate the assertion as well as the authority represented in the assertion)
  - Elaboration
    1. Grounds (supporting evidence for the reasons and the assumptions)
    2. Limits (constraints the arguer would place on the claim)
  - Anticipated reactions (potential responses from others holding diverse positions)
    1. Cooperative or supporting assertions
    2. Competitive or opposing assertions
    3. Altogether different assumptions
    4. Challenges to reasons or to grounds

The outline does not include rebuttal. A position paper should not rebut. Rather, it should state its reasoning in a way that shows that reactions to the writer's reasoning have been anticipated.

Task #2. Write the position paper

Review the Method in chapter 2 before you write to get the rhetorical framework for your document in mind.

By consciously thinking about your position in relation to others (*Strategy,* above) and outlining the logic of your argument (Task #1, above), you have already begun to plan the contents of the document. That does not mean that the document's contents should simply fill in the outline, however. Think of the outline as a skeleton. The contents are its body, clothed for a particular occasion.

The message that the document conveys will be your claim or your answer to the issue question.

When arguing in a policy context, you must be aware of your authority for making a claim. Authority in argument has two meanings, a practical meaning and a conceptual meaning. In practical politics, authority means credibility and power. Credibility derives more from a role than from a credential such as specialized expertise, although that might be relevant. (The phrase "consider the source" evokes this meaning of authority.) Any role carries its own kind of power, whether it's the power of elected or appointed office or the power of citizenship or community membership. Conceptually, authority means persuasiveness. Authority in this sense is a function of evidence and analysis. Authoritative writing convinces by the quality of its support for claims and its care for using information reliably. (The phrase "you can rely on it" evokes this meaning of authority.) The best policy arguments are both credible and persuasive.

The document must clearly show whose position it communicates. Yours? That of an organization that you represent? You must anticipate reactions to your position. Go back to the list you made of positions other than your own (see *Strategy*, above). To each position on the list, add the reaction you might accordingly expect, and then rank the reactions in order of importance to you. Anticipate responses, but do not rebut them in the position paper (unless you are directed to do so). Keep the focus on your position.

Condense greatly, for now. You will likely have later opportunity to elaborate. However, keep this in mind: ignoring information your readers may ultimately decide (under the influence of other arguments) is important will cost you credibility. Put detailed evidence in an appendix. Charts, tables, other graphics, or extended textual materials should normally be appended. However, the choice to append important details should rest on knowing the circumstances in which the position paper will be read and used. Writers especially should know whether all readers will see the entire document, including appendices. Use a standard citation style for identifying sources. Modern Language Association (MLA) style or American Psychological Association (APA) style might be sufficient.

If you are authoring a position paper that speaks for a group or organization, plan to allow adequate time for consultation. Are you the sole author, or do you have collaborators? Are you ghostwriting for someone else? Plan also to allow for review and revision, possibly multiple reviews calling for multiple revisions. Who will review drafts? Who will make revisions? Remember to check the final draft against expected standards (checklists, chapter 2) and revise further, if needed, before releasing.

Two Examples

To show argument on a common problem from a global perspective, examples from national U.S. policy and from African regional policy are presented next, below. The common problem is the need to reduce the social and economic vulnerability of poor and marginalized populations. Each example is followed by an outline (Task # 1, above) showing its policy argument.

Example 1 is presented elsewhere (chapter 3, Example 4) to illustrate problem definition. In this chapter it is presented again to illustrate policy argumentation. If you remember the contents from reading the document earlier, skip to the outline following.

Example 1.

Expanding the EITC for Single Workers and Couples without Children (aka tax relief for low-wage workers)

A Policy Brief prepared for the Center on Poverty, Work and Opportunity at the University of North Carolina at Chapel Hill

January 2007

Abstract
The Earned Income Tax Credit (EITC), the nation's largest anti-poverty program, now provides tax benefits of roughly $39 billion dollars a year to over 21 million households. By supplementing the earnings of low-wage workers, the EITC "makes work pay." The EITC's popularity can be attributed to its providing both work incentives and tax relief. In 1993, Congress extended a small earned income credit to singles and childless couples; however, about 96 percent of EITC dollars still go to families with children. This discussion paper argues that, while the emphasis of the EITC on rewarding work for families with children deserves continued primacy, expansion of the EITC to childless

single workers and married couples without children deserves greater attention for the following reasons:

- The disproportionate and growing income tax burden (payroll, sales, excise) faced by this group of workers;
- The growing segment of workers at the bottom of the labor market, particularly single men with low levels of education and training, who remain confined to low-wage jobs;
- The strict separation in our thinking between households with and without children requires reexamination, given the growing number of children with non-custodial parents; and,
- With a national savings rate below zero, the need to facilitate asset building for all low-wage workers, including those without children.

We recommend expanding the EITC for single workers and childless married couples with a range of policy recommendations, each targeting specific new subgroups of EITC recipients and addressing a slightly different purpose:

1. Increase the EITC from 7.65 percent to 15.3 percent of earnings up to $8,080 in order to directly offset payroll taxes; and adjust the phase-in and phase-out ranges;

2. Lower the age requirement for single and childless workers to qualify for the EITC from 25 to 21 to target greater workforce participation incentives to young workers just entering the labor market and making major decisions about work;

3. Encourage single low-income workers to claim the Advance (monthly) EITC and use the increase in employee payroll earnings to contribute toward health care insurance premiums; and,

4. Link the EITC to asset building options such as matched savings accounts for education and training, homeownership, retirement, and entrepreneurship. In addition, remove asset limits for other public benefit programs, particularly to assist those with disabilities to enter the labor market and build assets.

Introduction

The Earned Income Tax Credit (EITC) is a refundable federal income tax credit first enacted with bipartisan political support in 1975. The EITC encourages low-income workers with children to enter and remain in the labor market by supplementing the earnings of those working for low wages, thus "making work pay." [Additional content omitted.] In this policy brief, we explore three questions:

1. What do existing policy research and current data tell us about whether the original two goals of the EITC—payroll tax relief and encouraging employment—are being met adequately for the sub-groups of childless single and married workers;

2. Are there additional rationales that would justify an expansion of the EITC for this sub-group; and,

3. What policy changes could accomplish all or some of these policy goals?

[Additional content omitted.]

Summary of Key Findings
[Additional content omitted.]

- The disproportionate tax burden faced by low-wage single workers, which has worsened since the EITC was enacted in 1975, make tax relief an even greater priority as an issue of tax fairness. [Additional content omitted.] If any workers need a tax cut, we argue that these workers do.

- A growing segment of workers at the bottom of the labor market...remain confined to low-wage jobs...Leaving this group at the margins of the labor market undermines the strength of the workforce, communities, and families.

Additional Rationales for Expanding the EITC for "Childless" Workers:
In addition to the need for the EITC to better meet the goals of tax relief and encouraging work for childless workers, we also identified three additional reasons why an expansion of the EITC is warranted:

- Given changes in family structure and the growing number of children with non-custodial parents, the strict separation in our thinking between households with and those without children requires reexamination...

- Single workers who now qualify for the very modest credit can receive few if any other government benefits...

- With the national savings rate at zero, innovative approaches that promote savings and asset building for all low-income workers deserve support....

Policy Options for an Expansion of the EITC for Childless Workers

[Additional content omitted.]

Politically, at both the federal and state level, an expanded EITC could embody both progressive and conservative values by: (1) rewarding those who work with an earnings subsidy; (2) providing the greatest benefits to those with the greatest need; (3) offsetting the tax burden on working poor singles and childless married couples struggling to make ends meet; (4) providing incentives for people to enter the workforce who otherwise might not do so; (5) achieving these ends without increasing employer costs, without creating hiring disincentives and with minimal government bureaucracy; and (6) helping single workers and families without children, and potentially many more, to build assets for homeownership, education, and retirement when combined with other institutional supports such as matched savings programs....

Analysis and Policy Proposals

[Additional content omitted.]

Conclusions and Suggestions for Policy Reform

[Additional content omitted.]

(This is an extracted version of the briefing paper. To read the whole document including footnotes, tables, charts, appendices, and references, go to http://www.law.unc.edu/documents/poverty/publications/gittermanpolicybrief.pdf.)

Example 2.

Social Protection Statement by UNICEF Eastern and Southern Africa Regional Management Team

Background

While policies to promote broad-based economic growth are fundamental to overall social development, the benefits of growth do not automatically reach the poorest and most marginalized families; direct interventions are still required to reach the socially and economically excluded. Consequently, creating and strengthening social protection systems is an important priority for governments, donors, United

Nations (UN) agencies, and Nongovernmental Organization (NGO) partners in Eastern and Southern Africa (ESAR). Child welfare and protection concerns are often at the heart of these social protection efforts, requiring UNICEF to inform policy, practice, and advocacy in this area. Long considered a privilege of developed countries, social protection is now recognized for the role it can play in addressing poverty and vulnerability in developing countries. Among some development partners, social protection is considered part of the essential package of basic social services that the state ought to provide to its citizens.

The Livingstone Accord (March 2006) represents a major political landmark for social protection in the region. Thirteen countries in ESAR, under the auspices of the African Union (AU), have committed themselves to developing national social protection strategies, and integrating them into national development plans. Preparations for a Pan-Africa "Livingstone II" have just begun...[T]he AU will be developing a social protection position paper over the next 12 months.

A conceptual framework for social protection
[Additional content omitted.]

A comprehensive social protection system should include four broad sets of interventions:

1) Protective programs...offer relief
2) Preventive programs...avert deprivation...or mitigate
3) Promotive programs enhance assets...
4) Transformative interventions...address power imbalances...

Rationale for UNICEF engagement in social protection
...Critical are articles of the international covenants to which ESAR countries are signatories...[Additional content omitted.]

- Child protection and social protection
  - UNICEF defines child protection as "preventing and responding to violence, exploitation, and abuse..." [Additional content omitted.]
- Child sensitive social protection
  - Social protection should address both income poverty and social vulnerability, but we recognize that for children in particular, social vulnerability is especially important...[Additional content omitted.]

The major building blocks of child and gender sensitive social protection

Beyond the core principles articulated above, UNICEF identifies five key social protection interventions. [Additional content omitted.]

- An agenda for action
- [Additional content omitted.] UNICEF commits itself to working with governments and development partners to advance…social protection systems within the twenty countries in Eastern and Southern Africa. Specific work will be grouped into four cross cutting areas…A full matrix of milestones and country-level baselines are presented in the Social Protection Strategy document. [Additional content omitted.]

Conclusion

Social protection has not been a significant part of the international policy dialogue in Africa in the last 30 years…Nevertheless, given the political commitment already demonstrated at Livingstone by thirteen ESAR countries, …it is not overly optimistic to believe that significant results…can be achieved in the next 2–5 years.

(This position paper is abstracted from a larger social protection policy paper written by the UNICEF's Eastern and Southern Africa Regional Office entitled "Social Protection in Eastern and Southern Africa: A Framework and Strategy for UNICEF." The larger paper can be found at http://www.aidsportal.org/Article_Details.aspx?ID=9029).

What these examples show. Both position papers exhibit strong authoritative argument that is credible and persuasive. That strength is partly attributable to carefully constructed policy logic. An outline (Task #1, this chapter) showing the policy logic of each is shown here, below. The outlines refer to the extracted versions presented here. To fully appreciate the papers' argumentation, read the complete text accessible at the locations cited for each document. Keep the outline in mind as you read.

Outline of the Argument to Expand the Earned Income Tax Credit (EITC) in the United States

Problem: EITC eligibility limited to families with children.

Issue: Ineligibility of single workers and couples without children.

Question: Should EITC cover single workers and couples without children?

Claim: The EITC should be expanded to childless single workers and married couples without children for multiple reasons.

Support: Justification, elaboration, and limits

- Justification
  - Reasons
    - The disproportionate and growing income tax burden (payroll, sales, excise) faced by this group of workers;
    - The growing segment of workers at the bottom of the labor market, particularly single men with low levels of education and training, who remain confined to low-wage jobs;
    - The strict separation in our thinking between households with and without children requires reexamination, given the growing number of children with noncustodial parents; and,
    - With a national savings rate below zero, the need to facilitate asset building for all low-wage workers, including those without children.
  - Assumptions
    - Original policy goals of the EITC are to provide work incentives and tax relief for low-wage workers.
    - The present tax code is unfair to low-wage workers.
    - Progressive and conservative values support a safety net for people who work hard and play by the rules.

- Elaboration
    - Evidence for reasons
        - Empirical research on tax burden, job patterns, household demographics, and assets of low-wage workers
    - Evidence for assumptions
        - Legislative history showing intent of original EITC legislation and amendments from 1975 to present
        - Policy analysis of tax code
        - Political analysis of values (e.g., equity, efficiency, role of government)
- Limits
    - Political climate at the time of introducing a proposal to expand EITC
    - If adopted, speed of implementation
    - Coverage (recommended solution does not cover single workers who are noncustodial parents)
    - Anticipated reactions:
        - Cooperative (others might propose compatible policy changes, such as providing incentives for businesses to offer infant day care)
        - Competitive (others might argue that there are more pressing priorities, or there are better policy instruments, or for a different solution)
        - Different assumptions (replace the present tax code with a flat tax)
        - Challenges (need more empirical research and policy analysis before concluding that the tax code is unfair to low-wage workers)

Outline of the Argument for UNICEF Involvement in Creating Social Protection Systems in Eastern and Southern Africa

Problem: Poverty and marginalization in the region

Issue: Survival, development, and protection of vulnerable people, especially children

Question: Should UNICEF participate in the creation of national social protection systems in African Union countries?

Claim: UNICEF should participate

Support: Justification, Elaboration, and Limits

- Justification
  - Reason
    - UNICEF's commitment to the human rights based approach to development includes a commitment to the most vulnerable and marginalized, that is, those most in need of social protection.
  - Assumptions
    - Human rights principles
    - Economic efficiency arguments
- Elaboration
  - Evidence for reason
    - UNICEF's mission and history of activity in Africa
  - Evidence for assumptions
    - International covenants on human rights and children's rights to which ESAR countries are signatories
    - Demonstrated impoverishing effects of market failures
    - Demonstrated capacity-building effects of human investment
- Limits
  - Factors beyond UNICEF's control (magnitude of need, strength of national commitment, donor interest)
  - Anticipated reactions
    - Cooperative (participating governments will initiate programs)
    - Competitive (some governments will not participate)
    - Different assumptions (markets, not states, reduce poverty)
  - Challenges (demonstration of UNICEF's capacity to support national strategies)

In addition to their usefulness for writers and readers of position papers, outlines such as these can be used for briefings in policy workplaces.

Summary and Preview

Persuasive policy argument is purposeful, audience-aware, logical, and authoritative. This chapter implicitly tells you that positions supported by argument are more persuasive than unsupported opinion. It explicitly shows you how to argue policy positions professionally. Chapter 6, next, applies argument to requesting action.

Reference

Coplin, W. D., and M. K. O'Leary. 1998. *Public policy skills.* 3rd ed. Washington, D. C.: Policy Studies Associates.

Further Reading

Toulmin, S. 1958. *The uses of argument.* New York: Cambridge UP.

Petitions and Proposals: Request Action or Propose Policy

Key Concepts

- Getting government to act on your concern
- Requesting administrative action
- Proposing legislative action

Nongovernmental groups, as well as individuals, may request government action or propose public policy. Professionals in government may do so, too. This chapter shows you how to petition or propose in order to achieve policy change.

In the United States, only elected legislators are authorized to enact laws. However, requests for action and policy proposals may originate inside or outside government. While it is true that legislators or administrators originate most proposals, any citizen or group can petition for action or propose policy. Examples at the end of this chapter illustrate the variety of originators.

One longstanding practice for requesting action is petitioning. The First Amendment to the U.S. Constitution guarantees citizens' right to "petition their national legislature for a redress of grievances." Over time, petitioners have come to include not only individual citizens but also groups, organizations, and corporations of many kinds. Petitioning has extended beyond redressing grievances to requesting varied actions.

To illustrate petitioning, in a case of injury experienced during air bag deployment in an automobile collision, three different petitions for government action might be made.

1. A victim of chemical burns or breathing disorders attributable to air bag deployment might petition his congressional representatives to amend the National Traffic and Motor Vehicle Safety Act of 1966 to authorize medical training programs specific to air bags for emergency services personnel.
2. A company that has developed a new technology for increasing passenger safety without relying solely on passenger restraints, such as air bags or safety belts, might petition the National Highway Traffic and Safety Agency to test the new technology.
3. A professional association of automotive engineers might petition the National Highway Traffic and Safety Agency to amend a vehicle safety design standard to include warning systems in cars to encourage seat belt use.

The other common practice for requesting action is proposing policy. External proposals usually represent organized, or group, interest in solving a problem. The role of nongovernmental groups in North American public policy making has deep historical roots. In colonial America, before the United States or its government was established, voluntary associations flourished. Individuals formed associations to provide basic social services, to meet public needs, and to protect community interests. Voluntary fire companies, water companies, library associations, prison associations, school associations, landowner associations, and militias were so common in the America of the early 1800s that a visitor from France, Alexis de Tocqueville (1945), observed,

> Americans of all ages, all conditions, and all disposition constantly form associations.... Wherever at the head of some new undertaking you see the government in France, or a man of rank in England, in the United States you will be sure to find an association (106).

Such group activism provides background for the Tenth Amendment regarding limitations on central government that states "the powers not delegated to the United States by the Constitution, nor prohibited to it by the States, are reserved to the States respectively, or to the people."

Nowadays, groups that perform a public good might be granted tax-exempt status as nonprofit organizations. Their function might be religious, scientific, literary, educational, promotional, protective, political, charitable, or other, in accordance with Internal Revenue Service standards for twenty categories of tax-exempt activity (Internal Revenue Service 2002). Now, over a million nonprofit organizations operate in the United States (The New Nonprofit Almanac IN BRIEF 2002).

Many (possibly most) nonprofit organizations are not concerned with public policy. However, significant numbers of such groups actively try to influence the direction public policy takes. These are known as advocacy groups. Their methods vary according to the limitations of their tax-exempt status. Some limit their activity to education. These educate their members, the larger public, and the government regarding issues, but they do not lobby or support candidates for election. Their communications include legislative alerts, editorials and letters, personal visits to lawmakers, witness testimony, and more. Others, with more restricted tax benefits, might campaign for candidates running for office or lobby for outcomes of a process or provide lawmakers with expert information and political assessments and, on occasion, drafts of legislation.

Legislators often appreciate the help of advocacy groups in educating the public about needs for policy. Government staffs appreciate informed, accurate, well-argued lobbying because it helps them to brief legislators on complex or controversial issues. And, legislation and regulation writers might also appreciate proposed wording. (Example 1, this chapter, illustrates.) A positive example of public good resulting from such help might be the continued strengthening of legislation in the United States on smoking as a health problem. Past legislation on smoking has been passed in large part because healthcare advocacy groups worked with responsive legislators at all levels of government and educated the public to support directed warning labels on cigarettes, nonsmoking restaurant sections, and smoke-free public facilities. A negative example is the influence of lobbying by corporations and advocacy groups to weaken laws on occupational health and safety or on environmental protection.

The milk labeling case in chapter 1 exemplifies both positive and negative lobbying.

Grassroots organizations such as neighborhood or block associations, community clubs, workplace voluntary groups, and student organizations might also use petitioning or proposing to accomplish their advocacy, just as nonprofit organizations might.

Why are petitioning and proposing important? They sustain democracy; they are democratic ways of addressing public problems by institutional means. Whether by direct democracy (as with California's state referenda) or by representative democracy (as with Washington's federal legislation), self-governing society relies on procedures for public intervention in the process. Recall that public policy has far-reaching effects in the everyday life of society. Policy makers need and want information that can solve problems and build public support for action. Nongovernmental groups or individuals who are informed about the impact of a problem or a policy are excellent sources of information. So are groups or individuals who recognize a need for policy. Who petitions and proposes? Individuals can do so, but petitions and proposals by organized groups are likely to be more influential because they represent the power of collective interest.

How to Ask for Action or Propose Policy on Behalf of a Group

Goal: Knowledge of the functions of nongovernmental organizations in public policy processes, and familiarity with nonprofit organizations active in your area of interest.

Objective: Petitioning or proposing on behalf of an organization or group.

Product: Brief written petition or policy proposal representing an organization's advocacy. Length varies according to purposes and situations, but a short document (one to three pages) is preferred. Genre may be prescribed or chosen. A letter is a common choice.

Scope: Content of group's charter, purpose, or mission will determine the concerns or issues you will address.

Strategy: Create petition or proposal including the following information:

- Desired outcome: What do you want to accomplish? Can you describe it as if it were already accomplished in a future you want to achieve?

- Today's situation: What's wrong in the present? Why is the action you propose needed? What causes the need?

- Relevant background: How did the problem arise? What original assumptions are no longer valid? What conditions have changed?

- Available options: What are the alternative ways of meeting the need? Advantages and disadvantages of each? Costs (money, other) of each?

- Recommended action: What is the best alternative? Can you briefly argue as to why?

- Summary: What are the results (referring to the desired future) if requested action is performed?

- Action items: Who is asked to do what, when, where, and how?

Task #1. Name the need, and specify the action and agency

Identify a need for policy: If you already know the need you will address or the option you will advocate, proceed to the next step, specifying the desired action and the responsible agency.

If you do not know the need well, or if you have not decided on an option or you are responsible for selecting among many competing needs and options, step back to focus before you proceed. Start again wherever you need to start, whether it is to define the problem and pinpoint the issue (discovery), review the history of action or inaction (legislative history), review the arguments (the range of positions), or use the Method in chapter 2 to reconsider the policy context and the communication situation for your proposal.

Specify the action and agency: Determining the needed action—knowing what is possible, knowing whom to ask, and knowing what to ask for—is not simple. Much time and effort can be wasted in seeking unlikely action or making a proposal to the wrong recipient. The best way is to continually and iteratively ask and answer, "What am I trying to do?" and "How can I do it most effectively?" That will lead to further guiding questions such as "Should I start small (that is, local), or should I start big (national or international)?"

Consider the options for action; for example, choose government action. What do you want the government to do? <u>Government can legislate, spend, regulate, and enforce</u>, all within limits. Which type of action is needed for the problem you are concerned about? To which level of government—federal, state, local—should you direct your proposal? Which department or agency can do what you want to accomplish?

Now consider nongovernmental options. Does the solution require government action at all? For example, a citizens group might choose to organize a boycott or initiate a lawsuit to solve a civic problem rather than to ask for government action or propose public policy. Similarly, a student group might choose a community solution rather than governmental action. For example, in response to a racist incident on campus, one student group developed a constructive plan for educating students about everyday racism in campus life. Rather than proposing it as a policy to the student governance or to the school's administration, the group circulated their plan among other campus organizations and sent it to national student associations. They communicated it by word of mouth and publicized it through news media. The strategy was to ask similar student groups nationwide to draw public attention to the problem of race-based harassment on their campus and to offer as a model the original group's plan for addressing it. In this example, change in human behavior was sought through organized community education.

Task #2. Identify the organizations active on your issue

Here are some ways of locating and identifying nonprofit organizations:

- Check the local phone directory, or ask local volunteer services about local nonprofits or local affiliates of national and international nonprofits.

- Ask a librarian for print or online guides to nonprofit organizations. (Chapter 4 on legislative records research includes a reminder that research librarians are a real resource for communicators. A reference librarian specializing in management and business, for example, will know the latest print and online sources of information on nonprofit organizations.)

- Read the transcripts of congressional hearings on your issue to find witnesses who spoke on behalf of advocacy groups (To find hearings, see chapter 4 on legislative history and chapter 8 on witness testimony.)
- Search newspaper databases for news articles on your issue that might refer to advocacy groups.
- Search World Wide Web portals to nonprofit organizations. Some offer free searchable lists of nonprofits such as the following:
  - Institute for Nonprofit Organization Management http://www.usfca.edu/inom/index.html
  - Nonprofit Online News: http://news.gilbert.org
  - Internet Nonprofit Center: http://www.nonprofits.org
  - Nonprofit Yellow Pages http://www.nonprofityellowpages.org/ypsearch.asp
  - idealist.org: http://www.idealist.org
  - Independent Sector: http://www.independentsector.org
  - The Foundation Directory Online: http://lnps.fdncenter.org
  - Guidestar: http://www.guidestar.org

Why restrict your knowledge to that provided by nonprofit organizations? You should not necessarily limit your knowledge to a single kind of source. If, for example, you represent a healthcare organization and are advocating for the right to use a controversial drug, you may want to enlist the support of the pharmaceutical company that manufactures the drug. While the company has a vested interest, it also might have facts and figures that could bolster or undercut your arguments. As another example, if you are advocating for highway safety improvement, you might consult with both nonprofit and forprofit experts in accident research, such as the petitioners in Examples 1 and 2 (this chapter).

Task #3. Write

Absolutely key in petitioning and in proposing is providing only accurate information. Anything else will destroy your or your organization's credibility and persuasiveness.

Use the Method in chapter 2 to prepare, plan, and produce a written petition or proposal. The document's contents should answer the questions listed under *Strategy* (this chapter). Compare the finished product to expected standards (checklists, chapter 2).

There is no typical format for policy proposals. As noted in *Product* (this chapter), if you are writing for an organization that prescribes a template for policy proposals, you should use that template. If no template is prescribed, choose a form that is appropriate for your situation. For any written document requesting government action, the conventions of professional communication will apply. Identify the presenter and recipient, summarize in an overview, and organize content in subheaded sections. The document type might be a letter, a memo, a full-page ad in print newspapers, animated ads in online newspapers, a public declaration dramatically delivered in historical costume, a YouTube video, or another form chosen for its effectiveness in the situation. See, for example, the websites of national nonprofit groups that sometimes express their advocacy in funny as well as serious and attention-grabbing ways.

Four Examples

These examples show petitioning and proposing by internal governmental and external originators.

Example 1. Petition

Center for Auto Safety
1825 Connecticut Avenue, NW #33a
Washington, DC 20009-5708 (202) 328-1770
www.autosafety.org

January 21, 2007

The Honorable Nicole R. Nason, Administrator
National Highway Traffic Safety Administration
400 Seventh Street, SM7
Washington, DC 20590

Petition for Rulemaking

Dear Ms. Nason:

The Center for Auto Safety (CAS) petitions the National Highway Traffic Safety Administration (NHTSA) to take action to restrict the availability of two-way communication features through in-vehicle telematic systems while a vehicle is in motion. The purpose of this petition is to make the driving environment safer by reducing the availability of devices that have been proven to be traffic hazards.

According to NHTSA spokesman Rae Tyson, "Our recommendation is that you should not talk on the phone while driving, whether it's a hand-held or hands-free device." It is time for NHTSA to put the results of extensive research and its own recommendation into action.

Background

The automotive industry has long been aware of the dangers posed by talking on a cell phone while operating a motor vehicle. Cellular telephones are an important resource for drivers who encounter emergency situations and pull off the road to make calls. However, when cell phones are used while driving, they are a significant cause of highway crashes. Many existing in-vehicle technologies…are being expanded to offer cellular telephone service to drivers. What was once an essentially helpful technology is becoming a source of dangerous driver distraction by the addition of personal communication features that are available to a person while driving.

In search of new profit centers, major auto companies are marketing vehicle-in-motion telematic options that degrade the safety value of the Automatic Crash Notification (ACN) originally installed in motor vehicles. For example, General Motors, which was a leader in ACN with its OnStar system, began degrading safety by including personal cell phone use as an integral part of OnStar. GM once tried expanding the scope of in-vehicle telematic systems to allow drivers to receive email, movie listings, personalized news, sport reports and weather while driving. The potential distraction is similar to permitting television monitors in the front seats of passenger vehicles, a practice that is *not* permitted by state law in most, if not all states.

[Additional content omitted.]

Research Studies

Research has consistently shown that operating a motor vehicle while talking on a cell phone, whether hand-held or hands-free, increases the risk of an accident to three or four times the experience of attentive drivers. The general consensus of the scientific community is that there is little, if any, difference in crash rates involving hands-free versus hand-held cell phones. The two-way conversation on a cellular phone, not the task of holding the phone, causes a cognitive distraction. This distraction induces "inattention blindness," inhibiting drivers' abilities to detect change in road conditions.

State Legislation

[Additional content omitted.] The highest standard enacted by District of Columbia, Connecticut, New Jersey and New York prohibits the use of any handheld cellular phone but permits drivers to use hands-free wireless devices.

[Additional content omitted.]

Many cities have encountered difficulty enforcing bans because of the high number of violations...The total number of cell phone calls from 1996–2001, 326 billion, shows the enormous potential exposure of cell phone use in vehicles.

[Additional content omitted.]

Exemplary Vehicle Crashes

No one can deny that cell phones have resulted in traffic crashes, deaths, and injuries. [Name] and [Name] were both killed when drivers talking on cell phones struck their vehicles while they were stopped at a stop light.

[Additional content omitted.]

There are hundreds of cases like [theirs]...NHTSA has known from the time of the first head of the agency, William Haddon, MD, that the best public health strategy is one that is passive; in this case, not permitting cell phone technology to be so readily available.

Conclusion

[Additional content omitted.] It is time for the government to intervene on this dangerous practice...As a first step, the Center petitions NHTSA to issue a notice of proposed rulemaking which would amend FMVVSS102 to add a new provision reading:

Any vehicle integrated personal communication systems including cellular phones and text messaging systems shall be inoperative when the transmission shift lever is in a forward or reverse position.

[Additional content omitted.]

Sincerely,
Clarence M. Ditlow, Executive Director
Tyler Patterson, Vehicle Safety Intern

(The full petition can be seen at http://www.regulations.gov.
Docket ID: NHTSA-2007-28442
Document ID: NHTSA-2007-28442-0003
Date Posted: Sep 13, 2007)

Example 2. Petition

In the late 1990s, two professionals in auto safety created a forprofit corporation in the public interest to assist victims in litigation resulting from automobile accidents. Both are experts, one of them in highway safety policy and the other in automobile design for occupant safety. Concerned about the high rates of injury and fatality caused in part by drivers' and passengers' failure to use seat belts, the experts frequently petitioned the responsible federal government agency to amend the safety standard to require inducements in all vehicles to encourage seat belt use. Here, next, is a recent letter to the agency head regarding a persistent problem. This letter refers to earlier petitions by these experts. Following, a petition on the same problem with its transmittal letter to an earlier agency head is shown.

LETTER

Carl E. Nash
(address)
(phone)
(email)

February 11, 2002

The Honorable Jeffrey W. Runge, M.D.
National Highway Traffic Safety Administrator
Washington, D.C. 20590

Dear Dr. Runge:

As I promised at the Fuel Economy/Safety session of the Transportation Research Board meeting, I am enclosing copies of the petitions that Donald Friedman and I submitted to NHTSA before you became Administrator. They asked NHTSA to address the question of safety belt use inducements or reminders. We believe you, as Administrator, have considerable flexibility in how you might address this important contribution to motor vehicle safety.

NHTSA could take rulemaking action to require effective belt use reminders, but you could more expeditiously use your bully pulpit and other means to get auto makers to install more effective reminders in their new vehicles. A small research and fleet test program—which the industry should conduct along with NHTSA—could determine the most effective means of getting occupants to buckle up.

You are probably aware that the Insurance Institute for Highway Safety (IIHS) evaluated the weak reminder that has been included in most new Ford vehicles since 2000 and found that it increased usage by about five percentage points...Ford found no consumer resistance or complaints from this very innocuous reminder. A more effective reminder...could be developed with a modest research program. The safety payoff over the next decade would be quite substantial, not to mention the fact that it would free police resources now used to enforce belt use laws.

I am a strong advocate of non-regulatory approaches to automotive issues. In particular, the committee technical standards writing process of the American Society for Testing and Materials (ASTM) is highly democratic *(anyone with something to contribute can participate)*, effective *(it makes use of knowledge and expertise from all quarters)*, and fair *(it cannot be dominated by any specific interest and these committees must reach consensus)*. ASTM committees can produce consumer information standards that are objective, that meet the need for motor vehicle safety, and that are stated in performance terms. As an example, it would have been preferable to establish an (ASTM) committee to draft the side air bag standard last year.

[Additional content omitted.]

More comprehensive consumer information on motor vehicle safety can be an effective complement to NHTSA's minimum regulatory standards...This market-based approach is more flexible for both the government and auto makers, and can facilitate important choices by individual car buyers.

If you would like to discuss the possibilities of this approach further, I would be pleased to participate in such conversations and to recommend others with a similar interest in this approach.

With regards,
Carl E. Nash, Ph.D.
Enclosures

LETTER

Carl E. Nash
(address)
(telephone number)
(e-mail address)

December 17, 1998

The Honorable Ricardo Martinez, M.D., Administrator
National Highway Traffic Safety Administrator
400 Seventh Street, SW
Washington, D.C. 20590

Dear Dr. Martinez:

Enclosed is a petition for the National Highway Traffic Safety Administration to amend Federal Motor Vehicle Safety Standard 208 to require an effective safety belt inducement in all new motor vehicles. It has been a quarter century since the unfortunate experience with safety belt ignition interlocks. You have an obligation to seriously reconsider the potential of vehicle-based systems to substantially increase belt use.

The advantages of an acceptable, effective belt use inducement are substantial. It would reduce fatalities by at least 7,000 per year and would reduce injuries comparably. It would permit the agency to respond favorably to the industry's desire that NHTSA rescind the unbelted test in FMVSS 208. It would end the controversy over the use of safety belt use laws as an excuse for stopping minority drivers.

Donald Friedman and I have also submitted comments to the docket of the advanced air bag rulemaking notice that build on the concept of an effective safety belt use inducement. We believe that a simpler and more effective approach to reducing inflation induced injuries can be based on this concept.

In the interest of advancing motor vehicle safety, we look forward to your favorable consideration of our petition and of our comments on the rulemaking proposal. Action that could make belt use nearly universal in the United States is long overdue, and would be an important legacy of your tenure.

Sincerely,
Carl E. Nash, Ph.D.

PETITION

To Amend FMVSS 208, Occupant Crash Protection To Require Effective Belt Use Inducement

Carl E. Nash, Ph.D., and Donald Friedman
Washington, D.C., and Santa Barbara, California

Summary

This is a petition to amend Federal Motor Vehicle Safety Standard 208 (FMVSS 208) to require effective safety belt use inducement systems in all new motor vehicles sold in the United States. This requirement should become effective no later than the beginning of the 2001 model year. The inducement systems should activate only if a person sits in either front outboard seating position and does not attach the safety belt after occupying the seat and would stop when the belt is buckled. The requirement must be consistent with the "interlock" amendment to the National Traffic and Motor Vehicle Safety Act of 1966 (15 U.S.C. 1410b), which prohibits ignition interlocks and continuous buzzers.

The inducements could include, but need not be limited to: (1) a continuous visual warning to buckle safety belts located prominently on the instrument panel, (2) an intermittent, repeating audible suggestion (such as with a synthesized voice) warning occupants to buckle their safety belt, and (3) disruption of electrical power to such non-essential accessories as the radio, tape or CD player, and air conditioning. We further recommend that NHTSA undertake a quick reaction project to determine the acceptability and effectiveness of various types of use inducements to ensure that the spirit of the interlock amendment is not violated.

Background

[Additional content omitted.]

Restraint Policy and Use Today

[Additional content omitted.]

An Amendment to FMVSS 208

Therefore, we petition NHTSA to amend FMVSS 208 to require a reasonable and effective safety belt use inducement to be built into all new vehicles. Effective belt use inducements can be required without violating the "interlock" amendment (15 U.S.C. 1410b) to the National Traffic and Motor Vehicle Safety Act. [Additional content omitted.]

Safety belt use is widespread, generally accepted, and required by law in virtually all states. The design for comfort and convenience of safety belts in many new vehicles has improved since the days of the interlock. Thus, we doubt that many motorists would object to use of well-designed inducement systems. However, we recommend that NHTSA conduct quick reaction tests using panels and field tests to determine effectiveness and consumer acceptance of various types of use inducements. [Additional content omitted.]

We note that a policy of increasing belt use through an inducement built into new motor vehicles would be preferable to the present policy of safety belt use laws for reasons unrelated to safety. Civil rights organizations (most recently the Urban League) have objected to primary belt use laws because of their potential to give police officers an excuse to stop minority drivers. Having the inducement built into the vehicle takes away that issue and should be strongly supported by civil rights and civil liberties advocates.

Requiring a belt use inducement built into all new vehicles would be a major improvement in every way to FMVSS 208. As existing cars are retired from use, it would increase belt use to near universality (with the attendant reduction in fatalities and serious injuries in all crash modes) without further state laws or enforcement activities. In fact, states could sunset their safety belt use laws within the next decade or two. We estimate that a belt use inducement has the potential to save a minimum of 7,000 additional lives per year.

We urge that NHTSA give priority to both testing and simultaneous rulemaking in response to our petition.

(The full petition can be found at http://www.regulations.gov. Docket ID: NHTSA-1998-4405 Document ID: NHTSA-1998-4405-0062 Date Posted: Dec 17, 1998. For the agency's comment denying this petition see its *Federal Register* notice on advanced air bags: F.R. vol. 64, no. 214, page 60625–6. [The notice begins on page 60556]. The docket identifier is NHTSA 1999-6407-0001.)

What these examples show. Example 1 on cell phone use is an external petition by a nonprofit organization of experts. No specific policy process is underway, which explains why the petitioners ask the agency to start the process by issuing a notice of proposed rulemaking on the subject, use of cell phones while driving, and a call for public comment. Example 2, on seat belt use, also an external petition by a forprofit organization of experts, does address such a call.

Examples 1 and 2 illustrate in-depth presentation of information. They are written to be read silently, not spoken aloud. One cue to this intention is the length of sentences in both texts. Many sentences in Examples 1 and 2 would cause a speaker to run out of breath. Another cue is the extensive detail.

The amount of detail in Examples 1 and 2 is probably appropriate. For both petitions and proposals, as for funding requests, the contents and length of submissions might be prescribed by the receiving agency. If the agency prescribes the information and length it wants and the organization it prefers, write accordingly. Otherwise, a petition or proposal, like a grant application, might go unconsidered.

Where to put all the details? Putting them in the main body of the document can be an unwise choice. Detailed explication or historical background presented alongside your message can bury the message. A potential choice for the writers of Example 2 on seat belt use is to put explanation, background, and critique in an appendix. The success of this option depends on the circumstances of reception. To decide whether to append supporting information, writers need to understand the readers' situation. If all readers will receive the whole document and if they are willing to flip between the main text and appendix as they read, writers can safely choose to append detailed information. However, in some policy work settings, readers are likely to receive not the whole document but only the parts that pertain to their jurisdiction or responsibility. Appended information might not reach them. Perhaps the writers of example 2 on seat belt use knowingly chose not to use appendices.

Examples 1 and 2 are well organized for readability. Document structure aids rapid comprehension. Even so, the message could be emphasized more in Example 2. Within paragraphs, the petitioners' implicit message ("There is a better way") competes with the implied critique ("The agency's way is flawed"). Impatient readers might want a sharper focus on the message.

Example 3. Proposal

Scenario

Senior officers in the Surgeon General's Office have decided that another attempt to increase Reserved Armed Force eligibility for health care is justified. More frequent, longer lasting active deployments, increasing injury rates, and depleted state budgets for reservists' benefits motivate the new effort. The Chief of Patient Information has been persuasive, too. As anticipated, she is now tasked to write the necessary legislative documents. Collaboration with other specialist staff will be necessary. For example, as specialist for eligibility, she will gather dollar information and other numbers from the medical budget staff. When all information is in hand, she drafts a prescribed strategic planning document called a Unified Legislative and Budgeting Initiative (Example, below). Before it can be submitted to her immediate supervisor, all the peer specialists in her office with whom she has consulted will review the draft. Upon submission, it will be reviewed by an eight-level chain of command beginning with her immediate supervisor, going on to the Secretary of the Army and all applicable staff experts, Congressional liaison, and legal opinion to conclude, if necessary, with the Secretary of Defense. Any level of review may request changes, which she will make and then re-submit to the requesting reviewer.

FY 2011 Legislative Initiative
(Unified Legislation and Budgeting)

TITLE

Increase the Early Eligibility (EE) Period for TRICARE Benefits for Members of the Reserve Components

Short Proposal Description

To initiate a Unified Legislation and Budgeting (ULB) proposal to enable Reserve Components to address the Secretary of Defense's changes to mobilization policy. Under this proposal, the effective date for the entitlement to early TRICARE benefits for members of the Reserve Components receiving alert orders to active duty would be the date of the issuance of the alert order. Current law only provides 90 days of early TRICARE benefits for members of the Reserve Components. The current 90 day authorization does not provide sufficient advanced notice to allow Reserve Component members to take advantage of this benefit. This ULB does not propose a change to TRICARE coverage for military dependents or family members.

Approximate Full Year Cost ($M)

The current cost of this benefit to the government is $---- per service member, per year. [Additional content omitted.]

Discussion of Requirement and Relationship to HR Strategy

After a member is identified, screened and determined to be qualified for deployment, on average, he or she has a short time to take advantage of the Early Eligibility Period for TRICARE Benefits. If a member of the Reserve Components is identified as non-deployable due to a medical issue, the current 90-day TRICARE benefit does not provide adequate time for the medical issue to be treated. Additionally, the current benefit does not allow a service member adequate time to rehabilitate after medical treatment, thus eliminating a pool of otherwise deployable resources. As a result, the Reserve Components are overrun with service members who are unable to mobilize, leaving unit readiness diminished dramatically.

Providing an early TRICARE benefit upon the receipt of an alert order to active duty would allow for the treatment, rehabilitation, and successful mobilization for countless service members. This benefit will enable the fullest utilization of the service member's training and experience, to ensure higher levels of unit readiness. Extending this benefit will also solidify unit cohesion and allow the Reserve Components to be more responsive to wartime requirements.

This proposal would allow Reserve Component service members the maximum use of Early Eligibility for TRICARE. Increasing the eligibility period in coordination with other Reserve Component initiatives for earlier alert notification will result in higher unit readiness and higher retention of service members.

Business Case

Reserve Component service members do not currently have adequate time to utilize this benefit to identify, treat, and rehabilitate medically disqualifying issues prior to mobilization. This has a tremendous adverse impact not only on service members and their families, but more importantly, on unit readiness and national defense.

This proposal directly supports the Army Legislative Objective to reset the Force to ensure readiness for current and future challenges with full funding to restore units to levels of readiness required to successfully execute programmed operational deployments, future contingencies, and homeland defense missions.

This proposal will enable the reserve component service members to receive preventive care and treatments necessary to become fully medically ready. Extending this benefit to alert to mobilization will allow ample time during the Reset/Train Pool of the ARFORGEN cycle to increase the readiness percentage and bring the RAF force to a green status. In addition, this will allow leadership to focus on training, mobilization activities, increase unit readiness and most importantly increase the quality of life for the service member. DOD has a high interest is seeing a fully deployable RAF force.

All seven Reserve Components have a direct stake in seeing a change in the legislation for this benefit. The Army National Guard, the Air National Guard, the Army Reserves, the Air Force Reserves, the Marine Reserves, the Coast Guard Reserves, and the Naval Reserves would be greatly impacted.

Number of Personnel Affected

	Army	Navy	Marine Corps	Air Force
Number	54,000	6,000	4,000	12,000

Resource Requirement ($M)
The Early Eligibility for Medical Benefits (EE) is funded by the Defense Health Program Association Fund. Due to limited resources, the RAF does not have funding for this proposal.

[Additional content omitted.]

Note: This proposal requires a corresponding appropriation of funding for implementation.

Cost Methodology
Cost factors include 76,000 Reserve Component service members mobilized annually. The current cost of this benefit to the government is $--- per service member. (This data is based on the GAO TRICARE Reserve Select report 08-104, December 2007.) Currently there are 38,700

Soldiers deployed and eligible for this benefit. The estimated funding impact to provide twelve months worth of the EE benefit is $---M.

Legislative Language

Current Public Law 108–136, National Defense Authorization Act for Fiscal Year 2004, section 703 states "a member of the Reserve Components who is issued a delayed-effective date active duty order or is covered by such an order for a period of active duty of more than 30 days, in support of a contingency operation, as defined in 10 U.S.C. 101(a)(13)(B)., shall be eligible, along with the member's dependents, for TRICARE, on either the date of issuance of such an order, or 90 days prior to the date the active duty prescribed in the order, whichever is later."

This proposal will change Public Law 108–136 section 703 to read "...the effective date of active duty for purposes of entitlement to active duty health care of members of the Reserve Components of the Armed Forces receiving alert order anticipating a call or order to active duty in support of a contingency operation, shall be the date of the issuance of the alert order for the member's unit in anticipation of the mobilization of the unit for service for a period of more than 30 days in support of a contingency operation or the date of the issuance of the order providing for the assignment or attachment of the member to a unit subject to an alert order. The member's dependents shall be eligible for TRICARE 90 days prior to the date of active duty prescribed in the order."

This proposal does not impact any other section of the law.

Sectional Analysis
Pros

The proposal will dramatically improve medical readiness by allowing maximum time to identify and treat medical issues that may affect unit readiness and deployability.

Service members will have an increased ability to use the TRICARE Benefit throughout the entire alert period to identify and treat medical issues and to fully rehabilitate after medical treatment. This will ensure that Reserve Component units will be at a higher state of readiness and ensure the full use of each service member's skills and training.

Cons

The cost of this proposal is over $---- million over a five-year period. The RAF does not have funding for this proposal.

Example 4. Proposal

Scenario

An undergraduate student is a longtime volunteer in a local women's center that participates in a statewide coalition of private and public groups concerned about domestic violence. As a volunteer supporting the center's small administrative staff, the student is often given writing tasks. She has produced public information documents including brochures, guides to services, and how-to instructions. This time, her supervisor asks her to draft a policy statement on the center's advocacy for amending proposed legislation regarding guns and domestic abuse. The center director will present the statement in a public hearing on the legislation.

Policy Proposal

Who I Represent

For the past 20 years the Maryland Network Against Domestic Violence (MNADV) has been working to end domestic violence against women. MNADV works with domestic violence service providers and criminal justice personnel throughout the state to provide consistent community responses to domestic violence. In support of community response, MNADV focuses its lobbying efforts on changes needed in state law and has aided in passing almost thirty pieces of domestic violence legislation. Currently, we support the passage of HB1 46 Domestic Violence Protective Order Additional Relief. This legislation provides for legal procedures requiring domestic abusers to surrender firearms after a protective order hearing.

Our Position

The issue is whether a person who has been accused of an act of domestic violence should be allowed to own firearms. As a representative for MNADV, I am here to say that we strongly feel that keeping guns out of the hands of batterers will help prevent further physical injury to victims. In Maryland, the majority of domestic violence incidents involve a gun or other firearm.

Currently, Maryland has no law that keeps guns away from batterers. As a result, men who are convicted of domestic violence often end up going back to their victims, with a gun, when their sentence is over. If Maryland does not pass a law preventing batterers from owning firearms, victims who have survived are more likely to become victims again. If Maryland fails to pass such a law, the state is also failing to adequately protect abused women.

If a person convicted of or accused of domestic violence is charged with a misdemeanor for owning a firearm as HB 146 provides, the number of deaths due to guns in the case of domestic violence will be lowered.

What these examples show. Example 3 on military healthcare is an internal proposal by a professional in government. Example 4 on domestic violence is an external proposal by a volunteer in a nonprofit organization.

Example 3 shows use of a prescribed template for proposing legislation, while Example 4 shows an individually chosen form for making a public statement of advocacy. Example 3's pared-down style utilizes graphic devices, whereas Example 4's plain style utilizes to-the-point exposition. Each style fits its document's purpose and cultural context.

Because it is intended for oral delivery, possibly in a 1- or 2-minute summary, Example 4 on domestic violence is compact. It includes only the message and key evidence. In a public hearing, as in a briefing, time limitations usually force the omission of details from the oral statement. Details can be presented later in the hearing during question-and-answer. Details can be read, also, in the full written statement that is usually provided to the agency or committee holding the hearing. Additionally, a staff member for the hearing's convener might follow up by asking the organization's witness for more information.

Example 3 on military healthcare is intended to be read and discussed in meetings by people familiar with the genre, unified legislative and budgeting initiative, and with the subject, soldiers' health care needs. Consequently, it does not explain specialized terms such as TRICARE (current military health plan) or abbreviations such as FY2011 (fiscal year 2011).

Example 3's argument is strongly supported by evidence of need, examination of assumptions, legislative analysis, and political analysis.

All examples here are credible. Each, for its purpose, informs sufficiently and organizes content readably. Examples 3 on military healthcare and 4 on domestic violence do not provide accountability by naming the presenter and intended recipient in the document shown here. Likely, an accompanying cover sheet or other tracking sheet did name them.

Summary and Preview

Inside government, there might be a formal procedure for gaining policy makers' attention. Outside government, typically there is not such a procedure. Getting a problem on the public agenda is more an art than a science. This chapter introduces you to two common ways, petitioning and proposing. Chapter 7, next, adds skills for briefing policy makers.

References

Internal Revenue Service. *The Digital Daily.* 2 May 2002. <http://www.irs.gov>.

The New Nonprofit Almanac IN BRIEF: Facts and Figures on the Independent Sector. 2 May 2002. <http://www.independentsector.org>.

Tocqueville, Alexis de. 1945. *Democracy in America.* Vol. 2. 1840. New York: Alfred A. Knopf.

Briefing Memo or Opinion Statement: Inform Policy Makers

Key Concepts

- Brevity
- Politeness
- E-communication

Policy makers need information for making decisions. They usually prefer it in short, quickly comprehended summary form. This chapter helps you to write two kinds of summary, a briefing memo and an opinion statement. It includes cautionary guidance on email.

During a policy process, authorities receive large amounts of unsolicited information and advice. Often, they ignore it. Instead, they directly seek the information and advice they need.

What kinds of information or advice do policy makers typically need? For consideration of a problem, general information might include assessments of events or conditions; arguments and critical analyses of arguments; reviews of policy options and technical analyses of the options; specialized topic reports; investigative reports; summaries of laws germane to the issue; legal counsel on interpretation of laws; and summaries of expert opinion, public opinion, and political advocacy. Beyond these general types of information, any single issue demands its own particular and detailed information.

For example, a municipality that is developing a comprehensive plan for land use will need general assessments of area conditions (environmental, economic, historical, and cultural factors), reports on current costs of providing services in the area (such as roads, water, and sewage treatment), summaries of relevant state laws (such as regulations governing municipal planning), and more. To apply general information to a specific municipality (such as a township or village), its elected officials might ask county or state government agencies for local population statistics, economic projections, or environmental data. They might ask legal counsel to examine land-use planning tools, such as zoning ordinances in nearby municipalities, or to review case law on legal challenges to them. To prepare for public discussion of draft plans and ordinances, the officials will seek political advice. They will want to know the opinion and advice of organized groups and individuals living in the municipality.

Who provides information to policy makers? It varies by level of government. In federal and state governments, professional staff might produce much of the needed information. The staff's know-how, or familiarity with the policy process and understanding of the political context, enables them to inform policy makers usefully. Staff members typically write briefing memos. As distinguished from extensive memos, such as policy analysis memos (see chapter 3, Example 4), briefing memos are terse and targeted summaries of essentials.

Municipal government differs from federal and state government in the size of staffs. While large municipalities might be well staffed, smaller ones have small staffs, or no staff. Consequently, local elected officials might do their own information gathering. They might utilize a range of information providers including experts (representing subject knowledge), advocacy and stakeholder groups (representing organized interests), legal counsels (representing rules and procedures), other officials and associations of elected officials (representing politics), and citizens (representing the opinion or experience of individuals or groups). Any of these providers might write an opinion statement or a briefing memo to inform an official's work of representation.

A briefing memo provides succinct, pointed information to people who have too much to do and not enough time. Whether its topic is narrow or broad, a briefing memo offers only essentials targeted to a particular reader's need to know. As distinguished from policy analysis memos or policy briefs, which are longer and include discussion, possibly with detailed appendices, briefing memos are short and compact. They highlight, only. One to two pages is the expected length. Writers of briefing memos should design content for quick comprehension and easy referral. Pages should have a document header for targeted identification; an opening summary (not an introduction) for overview; "chunked" information with subheadings for directing attention; shorter sentences with one main idea per sentence for emphasis, and only necessary words.

How to Inform Policy Makers in a Briefing Memo or Opinion Statement

Goal: Recognition of meaningful information in a mass of details and representation highlighting the significance of information for a user.

Objective: Skills of distilling, listening, recording, observing, evaluating sources, relating details to context, interpreting details accurately in context, and selecting details according to relevance; capability of stating informed opinion that is aware of and responsive to other opinions.

Product: One- to two-page written briefing memo, or one- to two-paragraph written opinion statement, possibly with attachments.

Scope: Only essential topics in an identified context to target a specific information need.

Strategy: Use of guiding questions to develop the document's contents. All of the questions in the Method (chapter 2) apply.

Task #1. Develop the information

From meetings:

- Attend relevant public or private meetings; take full notes; get copies of the agenda and related documents; get contact information for participants.
- Jot (in the margins of the agenda) your own notes and questions about the proceedings, and capture (as nearly verbatim as you can) the significant questions asked by others.

- Contact participants, government staff, topic experts, or knowledgeable citizens for answers to questions or referrals to other sources immediately after the meeting.

From experts:

- Conduct information searches for relevant research and analysis.

From informed reflection and analysis:

- Update original questions and reframe the issues as information develops.
- Pause periodically to summarize your understanding and to critically examine it.
- Continue to consult as needed to improve your understanding of the process and context.

Task #2. Write the memo or statement

Before you write, review the Method in chapter 2. Tailor its questions to your purpose and audience.

Craft the document's contents for quick comprehension and ready use. Do not include everything you know; include only what the user needs and what the purpose requires. (You can provide more information later, if necessary.)

Choose the right presentation medium. If you are representing an organization, use its template (if it has one) for briefing memos. Communicate your memo or statement on the organization's letterhead stationary. If you are free to design the communication, fit it into one or two well-designed pages, as described earlier in this chapter. If the situation demands, you might also use a cover letter or attachments. Note: Before attaching anything crucial, consider the circumstances of reception, or how the document will be read and used. Attachments sometimes get detached when the document is circulated.

After drafting the communication, review and revise as needed (checklists, chapter 2). If you are pressed for time, revise only the overview to focus the message sharply. From the reader's perspective, that is most important.

Example 1.

This section presents a briefing memo written by a community resident to a local official. First, a scenario shows the context.

Scenario

Local government officials anticipate a farmer's request to operate a concentrated animal feeding operation (CAFO) in the municipality. It will be the first request of its type made since the municipality adopted a comprehensive plan for land use and a zoning ordinance. In that ordinance, although it is ambiguous, CAFOs may be considered as conditional uses of agricultural land to be permitted only if they meet site-specific conditions.

In preparation for reviewing the anticipated request and making a decision, the municipal official who chairs the planning commission begins to self-educate regarding CAFOs. His first objective is to become familiar with state law governing local authority to regulate CAFOs. He browses county and state government listservs; identifies technical and legal experts for possible consultation; attends relevant workshops, public hearings, and meetings; searches databases maintained by the state association of municipal officers and state government agencies; and searches municipal archives of public comment during the process of zoning adoption.

In a public meeting, he offers a preliminary interpretation of state law setting boundaries on municipal authority regarding CAFOs. A resident attending the meeting questions his interpretation. After the meeting, she offers to research the matter further. Given his lack of staff and the limited time he can devote to any single problem, he accepts her offer.

She locates the relevant state law and regulations online and reads them. She telephones state officials involved in authoring and implementing the regulations to ask about interpretations. They refer her to current case law on CAFOs and municipalities. Following up on their referrals and using the help of librarians in the state law school, she reads synopses of relevant current and pending cases.

Several days after the meeting in which she raised questions, she composes a one-page summary of findings and includes her interpretation of them. She emails the summary to the local official.

The sample briefing memo that follows was attached to an email message.

EMAIL MESSAGE

Doug,

I recognize that the township supervisors and planning commissioners are trying to operate within state law on CAFOs. It's a complicated task, and I appreciate the careful thought you are putting into it. My intentions are to help by getting good advice on interpreting state regulations so that we rightly know what authority Gregg Township has regarding CAFOs.

You raised two concerns in the July meeting of township supervisors. In the attached memo, I report what I've found and what I think regarding those two concerns. Basically, I find and I believe that the township has the necessary standing and authority to regulate CAFOs. You might want to talk to Douglas Goodlander (my source in Harrisburg). I'll call you later this week to see if you want to talk about any of this.

Catherine

ATTACHMENT

Memorandum
Summary
Gregg Township has "zoned in" the possibility of CAFOs, and it may regulate them within the limits of state law.

The Prohibition of CAFOs
You say, "You can't zone concentrated animal feeding operations out [prohibit them by means of zoning]." *Reference:* Pennsylvania State Association of Township Supervisors. See July issue of *PA Township News* for article "Avoiding Controversy: How Townships Can Minimize Conflicts between Residents and Intensive Ag Operations."

I say: Gregg has provided for the possibility of CAFOs operating in the township by making "feedlots" a conditional use in the agriculture zone. If "feedlots" can be construed to include CAFOs, then Gregg has "zoned in" the possibility. The zoning ordinance has a procedure for permitting, or not permitting, conditional uses based on case-by-case review for specified criteria. *Source:* Gregg Township Zoning Ordinance, Article 3, Agricultural Zone, Conditional Uses, C.4 Feedlots (p. 10), and Article 9, Conditional Uses, C. Criteria (pp. 3–4).

Municipal Regulation of CAFOs

You say, "I read the state regulation as taking the wind out of our sails in regulating CAFOs." *Reference:* The "pre-emption of local ordinances" provision of the Rules and Regulations, 25 PA Chapter 83 Subchapter D, 803.25 (b) for the Nutrient Management Act (3 P.S.1701 et seq.) published in the *Pennsylvania Bulletin,* Vol. 27, No. 26, June 28, 1997.

I say: municipalities can regulate CAFOs. The next section of 83.205 (part c) states that "nothing in this act or this subchapter prevents a municipality from adopting and enforcing ordinances or regulations that are consistent with/no more stringent than the state act." Beyond nutrient management [antipollution measures to prevent excess nutrients in animal manure from entering water sources], other issues presented by CAFOs such as odor, noise, air pollution, and road use can be locally regulated. *Source:* Douglas Goodlander of the Pennsylvania Conservation Commission. Goodlander is an author of 25 PA [nutrient management regulations] who has been involved in CAFO court cases in PA. He cautions that he can provide interpretation but not legal counsel. He encourages you to call him if you want (telephone number provided).

What this example shows. Two characteristics of this communication are especially noteworthy: its form and its intelligibility in context. Internet communications such as email differ in several ways from other written or spoken communications. Email is typically more informal and personal and often has less regard for spelling or grammatical correctness. In a public process, if taken out of its original context, email might embarrass the sender or recipient. Or it might compromise the action.

The intelligibility of this message relies on context. The sender and receiver know each other and have worked together before. They generally agree on the importance of local control in governance, but they might disagree on regulation of CAFOs. In the limited context of a policy process underway, they have been meeting and talking about this particular issue before this email was sent. When the email and its attachment are read together, they can be accurately understood in context. If they are read outside the context or if the two documents are separated and one is read without the other, the communication might be misinterpreted.

Why does this matter? Correspondence with an elected official is open to public scrutiny. In addition, the email and its attached memo will become part of a permanent public record. The elected official in this example is obliged to archive all communications on public matters and to make them available to anyone with a right to public information now or in the future. You may have seen cautionary evidence, such as the following notification at the end of a town officer's email:

> Pursuant to North Carolina General Statutes Chapter 132, Public Records, this electronic mail message and any attachments hereto, as well as any electronic mail message(s) that may be sent in response to it, may be considered public record and as such are subject to request and review by anyone at any time.

Context affects intelligibility in another way, too. If the two parts of the communication, the email and its attachment, become separated in a process of referring or forwarding the documents, the tone of either one might lead to misinterpretation. The brisk tone and terse wording of the memo might seem unfriendly. (Method, chapter 2, advises you to consider the attitude a communication might imply.) Contrasting viewpoints are summarized in efficient parallelism ("You say, I say"). Only necessary words are used. Citations and contact information are strategically included to save time for a busy official who does much of his own research. There is a downside to this efficiency, however. While its intention might be to help, the briefing memo's terse style lacks the sympathetic tone of the covering email that acknowledges the difficult problem the official must resolve. If the two documents are received separately, the reader's reception of either might be affected.

Communication is more than an information exchange; it is also a social interaction. The tone or implied attitude of a policy communication can affect its reception and possibly a working relationship. Recalling that policy makers receive lots of unsolicited communications, you should be aware that tone explains why some communications are ignored. Memos or statements that are expressly hostile or that seem closed-minded are not likely to be read, to receive a response, or to be useful to the process.

More Examples

Here are several more examples that illustrate good tone and bad tone in statements of opinion. These examples were emailed by citizens to an elected official in county government regarding a proposed merger of city and county schools.

Good tone. The following three opinion statements got the policy maker's careful attention and received a substantive reply.

A. You currently face a difficult decision regarding the proposed merger of [Town and County] Schools. I am writing to suggest a public referendum on this matter given the significant impact that the results of your decision will have on your constituency. Thanks for taking time to consider this request.

B. The merger discussion is heating up quickly, and I'm hoping the real issue of the disparate funding for the two systems doesn't get lost in the commotion. The push for a referendum, called for by so many [Town] parents, seems a veiled attempt to simply stifle discussion, allowing the real issue to again get swept under the rug, still unfixed.

C. Here are a few questions I'd love to have answered. I know you're busy and probably receiving hundreds (??!!) of emails daily on this issue. I hope you can fit me in.

1. Do you see a funding imbalance between the two systems?
2–7. [Additional content omitted.]

We need a solution. Thank you for considering my questions.

Bad tone. In contrast, the following three opinion statements (like many similar ones generated by a letter-writing campaign) got little attention and received no reply.

A. I understand that the [County] Board of Commissioners is evaluating a merger of the [Town and County] School Systems. I would like to communicate that:

1. I, along with most of my local colleagues and neighbors, are vehemently OPPOSED to a merger.

2. I request that a public REFERENDUM be held on this issue ASAP.

3. Unless proper procedure is followed throughout, a proposed merger will be challenged in the [State] and Federal courts to the extent necessary.

4. The voting records of the entire board will be well remembered and publicized in time for the next ELECTION.

B. I am greatly disappointed in your decision Wednesday night to short circuit democracy in our county. None of you ran last November with a position on school merger. You have suddenly sprung it on the citizens of the county. Since you would not face voters on the issue, you should allow a referendum on the issue in the county. Otherwise, you should delay the issue until an election year, and run on your beliefs. The idea that you can have a "stealth" merger of school systems and avoid the will of the citizens of the county, as some of you seem to believe, is not in keeping with the traditions of transparency and progressive politics in our county. I voted for you all last November. But I did not vote for school merger. Now I feel that your election was as much a sham. I would like a chance to vote on school merger or to vote again on your positions on the county commission.

C. I am very concerned about an article in the *Herald* which indicates that the schools in [County and Town] may merge. I don't understand what the advantage of such a move would be. If there is an advantage to the move please let me know what it is. If there is no advantage to the move, please let me know by ignoring this message.

What all these examples show. These examples teach ethical communicators to make careful choices. A public policy communicator has to make many competing choices. Purpose, contents, presentation style and tone, medium of delivery, and concern for immediate reception and use as well as the permanent record—all these must be considered and choices made. The choices are important because the consequences are significant. The outcomes of policy affect real people and places.

Summary and Preview

Information for a purpose and for targeted readers is characteristic in policy work. Opinion and information are vital to the process. This chapter focuses on two common ways of informing policy makers in a pointed manner. A briefing memo is the written equivalent of the spoken one-minute "elevator speech" or the one-minute oral summary of testimony. A statement of personal opinion is the equivalent of a voicemail message. Keep the tone of such communications professional and friendly, or at least neutral. Politeness is highly valued in the cultural context of public policy making.

In chapter 8, next, you'll learn about another way of informing policy makers that allows interaction, testifying as a witness in public hearings.

CHAPTER *8*

Testimony:
Witness in a
Public Hearing

Key Concepts

- Prepare to write and to speak
- Prepare to present a statement and to answer questions

Policy makers and administrators are required to deliberate publicly and to seek input. Witnesses provide input. This chapter prepares you to testify as a witness in a governmental public hearing.

In the U.S. federal government, "sunshine" or public access laws mandate open hearings for all legislative functions—making law, appropriating funds, overseeing government operations, investigating abuse or wrongdoing, and approving nominations or appointments to office. Hearings are held in executive and legislative branches of federal government. In state and local governments, public deliberation is mandated, but formal hearings are not as commonly held as at the federal level.

In government organized by a political party structure, the majority party (the party in power) chairs committees and thus sets the agenda for committee work, including public hearings. Committee chairs (with their staffs) decide whether to hold a hearing on a topic within their jurisdiction, what the purpose of a hearing will be, and who will be on the witness list. Topics and purposes of hearings reflect the committee's jurisdiction and the chair's political agenda. The agenda might or might not reflect cooperation between the majority and minority interests of members on the committee.

Several committees might hold hearings on different aspects of the same topic, especially if the topic concerns a hot issue that crosses jurisdictions. Hot issues are those that are currently in the news, controversial, or especially significant in some way. Most hearings are not about hot issues, however. Most hearings are workaday sessions to oversee government operations, to decide on appropriations of funds, to reauthorize programs, and so forth. They do the routine work of governance.

Public affairs television usually does not broadcast these routine hearings. Selected daily hearings are summarized on the government page of newspapers and some advocacy group websites. Some congressional committee websites broadcast hearings in progress.

In the executive branch, departments or agencies hold public hearings on issues within their regulatory responsibility. Some are held in the field, in geographic areas or political districts directly affected. Executive branch hearings vary in format from informal public meetings to formal deliberative sessions. The state environmental agency's hearing on water protection described in Example 2, below, illustrates informal field hearings in which executives, staff, and witnesses freely discuss a topic.

Taking U.S. congressional committee hearings as the model, hearings typically follow this order of events. After the chair opens the hearing, announces the purpose, and states his or her position on the topic, the committee members then state their positions and, possibly, their constituency's concerns regarding the topic. Next, invited witnesses testify on the topic. Following the testimonies, the usual practice is for committee members to question the witnesses.

In principle, anyone might be invited to testify who can provide information that lawmakers or administrators seek. In reality, witnesses testify at the federal level only by request of the committee. At state and local levels, the witness list is more open. There, you may be invited, or you may ask, to testify. If you wish to testify, you contact the staff of the committee or the agency holding the hearing.

In the communication situation of a typical hearing, witnesses testify as spokespersons for an organization or a government agency.

Occasionally, individual citizens testify on their own or their community's behalf. Witnesses must relate their special concerns to a policy context and their agendas to other agendas. Policy makers and witnesses interact face-to-face, and exchanges might be polite or confrontational. Questioning might be focused or loose. Questioning is always political, and sometimes it is bluntly partisan. The atmosphere might be orderly or hectic. The time limits are always tight—typically 1–5 minutes for each witness to present testimony and 5 minutes for each member to question all the witnesses. There might be multiple rounds of questioning. Hearings can last for hours or days if the committee or the witness list is large.

Legislative hearings are characteristically more freeform than legal hearings in administration of justice. In legislative hearings, generally, there are no prescribed rules for disclosing evidence or for objecting to questions as there are in law court hearings. Exceptions are investigative hearings in which witnesses might testify under oath. Even then, questioning is not constrained by rules. Consequently, witnesses for legislative hearings must prepare well for anticipated and unanticipated developments in the question-and-answer session that follows presentation.

Everything communicated in a hearing goes (via a legislative stenographer) into a transcript. This transcript is the official public record of the hearing. There are actually two public records, unofficial and official. Unofficially, the hearing might be broadcast and reported by news media followed by commentary in all media. These influential accounts shape public discourse and the perception of problems; however, they are not authoritative. They would not be included in a legislative history, for example. For the authoritative and official record of a hearing, a stenographer records the statements, questions, and answers verbatim, exactly as they are given. In current legislative reporting practice, the verbatim transcript cannot be edited, except to correct factual errors.

The transcript is later (sometimes months later) printed and published by the superintendent of government documents through the government printing office. This is the official, or legal, record of the hearing. Published hearing records are important for democratic self-governance because they give continuing public access over time to the accurate and full information produced by a hearing. That information is useful for many purposes. Journalists, law clerks, academic researchers in many fields, legislative staff, lobbyists, advocates, and active citizens use hearing transcripts as sources. Published hearings are primary sources for legislative history research, for example. They are also major sources for determining a law's original intent when the law is being adjudicated.

In the overall significance of government hearings for democracy, witness testimony is most important. For witnesses, it is an opportunity to bring concerns to the table, to talk directly with policy makers, to make personal or professional knowledge useful for solving problems. For policy makers, hearings offer a rare opportunity to talk directly with knowledgeable witnesses and to question them. Policy makers appreciate that interaction. Most information they receive is filtered through staff or advisors. They like having the chance to interact with other sources of information and perspective.

How to Deliver Oral Testimony Based on a Written Statement

Goal: To speak authoritatively and to answer questions responsively in public deliberation.

Objective: Skill of writing speakable text, skill of speaking easily from written text, and readiness to answer anticipated and unanticipated questions.

Scope: Pinpointed topic pertinent to a hearing's purpose and the witness's role.

Product: Two expected communication products are as follows:

- Short oral summary, either a list of talking points (outline for speaking) or a one-page overview (to be read aloud)
- Full written statement, possibly with appendices, to be included in the record of the hearing

Strategy: Confident and useful public testimony resulting from advance preparation.

Develop a Testimony in Context

Obviously, witnesses must know their subject and their message. More importantly, witnesses must understand the purpose(s) of the hearing and their own role and purpose(s) for testifying. Effective witnessing is achieved by presenting concisely and by responding credibly to questions. Responding to questions effectively is most important. If you are on the witness list, you are acknowledged as having something relevant to say. You do not need to impress people by showing how much you know about the topic. Focus strongly on your purpose and your message in relation to the hearing's purpose.

Know the context. To what policy process does the hearing relate? To what political agenda? Who's holding the hearing? What is the stated purpose of the hearing? What is the political purpose? Who else is on the witness list? What are their messages likely to be?

Know your message. Distill your message into one to two sentences that you can remember and can say easily. How does your message relate to the purpose of the hearing? How does it relate to other witnesses' messages? Anticipate committee members' responses and questions. What are you likely to be asked?

Know your role. Are you speaking for an organization? For yourself? Why are you testifying? What do the organizers of the hearing hope your testimony will accomplish?

Know the communication situation. Will the press attend the hearing? Are you available for interviews after the hearing? Will the hearing be televised? How is the hearing room arranged? Do the arrangements allow you to use the charts, posters, or slides? Are those visual aids a good idea if the room lights cannot be dimmed (due to televising of the hearing)? What is the location for the hearing? If you are using charts, posters, or slides, how will you transport them? Who will set them up in the hearing room?

Rehearse your delivery. Will you read your statement or say it? Generally, saying it is preferred. Be ready to do either, however. Rehearse by reading the full statement aloud and by speaking from an outline. You'll discover which way is easier for you and which you need to practice more.

Task #1. Write the testimony

Use the Method (chapter 2) to plan testimony in both oral and written forms. Some witnesses prefer to outline the oral summary first and then to develop the full written statement from that outline. Others prefer the opposite way. They write the full statement first; then they outline an oral summary based on the written statement.

The key to both? *Preparation.* Write out your oral summary, even if it is simply a list of talking points on an index card. The written list will provide confidence and control as you testify. Recall that everything said in a governmental public hearing is recorded and that the record is made publicly available. Do not plan to wing it or to testify extemporaneously. If you do that, you risk exceeding time limits, which committee chairs do not like. And you might forget important information, say more or less than you intend to have on the public record, or find yourself being asked questions (about something you said) that you are not prepared to answer.

If you are free to organize your testimony, you might want to use the following template. Use it in outline form for the oral summary, and expand it appropriately for the full written statement. Put extensive support in appendices, not in the main statement. (Both the oral and written versions will be included in the transcript of the hearing.) Here is the template:

- Title page or header to identify the organization and the witness, the agency holding the hearing, the topic, the date, and the location of the hearing
- Greeting to thank the organizers for the opportunity to testify and to state why the topic is important to the witness
- Message to state the main information the testimony provides
- Support (evidence, grounds) for the message
- Relevance of the message to the hearing's purpose
- Optional: discussion or background to add perspective on the message (only if relevant or if specifically requested by conveners of the hearing)
- Closing to conclude the testimony and invite questions

Task #2. Write the full statement

The written statement might use the same organization as the oral summary. The written statement may be longer, include more details, and be accompanied by appendices. It can be any length, but it should be no longer than necessary. Even if the written statement is lengthy, it must be organized and concise. That way, it is more likely to be read and used. Tip: good organization enables you to condense on demand if, for example, you are asked by the committee chair to limit your remarks. If that happens, present your message, state its relevance to the hearing's purpose, and conclude by saying that you will be glad to answer questions. Add omitted content in your answers to questions

Task #3. Present the testimony

The following tips are important.

- Summarize. During oral delivery, whether reading a document aloud or speaking from an outline, state only the essentials. Save the details for the question-and-answer period.

- State the message early and emphatically. Whether reading a text or speaking from an outline, state the message up front.

- Stay within time limits. Usually, the chair of a hearing will tell you the time limits. If not, assume that you have 2–5 minutes for a summary. Do not go over the limit.

- Listen. Closely attend to the opening statements by the committee chair and the committee members. Opening statements cue the questions that you might be asked. Or they might include content to which you want to respond later, when it is your turn to speak. Listen also to other testimonies. Committee members might ask you to comment on other witnesses' testimonies.

- Answer credibly. The question-and-answer time is often the most important part of a hearing. Committee members and witnesses alike agree on this. For committee members, it is a chance to interact directly with knowledgeable people. Members usually ask prepared questions to get important concerns, as well as witnesses' responses to the concerns, on the record. For witnesses, the question-and-answer time is a chance to connect their message to varied agendas represented in the questions or to pinpoint the usefulness of their knowledge to the committee. Witness effectiveness depends primarily on the witness's credible (honest, accurately informed, relevant) responsiveness to questioning.

After you have presented your testimony statement, shift your attention to question-and-answer communication. Follow these important guidelines:

- Listen to the questions asked of other witnesses. Do not daydream or otherwise lose focus while others are being questioned.

- Make sure you hear each question correctly when you are being questioned. If you are not sure you heard the question correctly, ask to have it repeated.

- Answer the question that is asked, not some other question that you half-heard or that you prefer.

- Stop when you have answered a question. Wait for a follow-up question. Postpone details, elaboration, or qualification on your original answer until a follow-up question allows you to provide them.

- Do not lie or invent information. If you hear yourself fabricating an answer (perhaps out of nervousness), stop. Politely ask to have your answer removed from the record, and begin again.

- Handle these situations especially carefully:

  - You are asked for your personal opinion. When you testify as spokesperson for an organization, be careful to present the organization's viewpoint. Avoid giving a personal opinion unless specifically requested, and then only if you appropriately can do so. If you do, be careful to distinguish your own view from the organization's.

  - You don't know the answer. Depending on the dynamics at the moment (neutral or friendly or confrontational) and considering the effect on your credibility of not answering, you might choose among these options: Simply say you do not know, say you are not prepared to answer but can provide the answer later, ask if you might restate the question in a different way that you can better answer, or defer to another witness who can better answer the question.

  - Your credentials are challenged, or your credibility is attacked. Do not get angry. Do not confront the challenger or attacker. Politely state your or your organization's qualifications to speak on the topic of the hearing. Restate why you are testifying or why the hearing topic is important to you or your organization. Maintain your role in the hearing as a source of information and perspective not offered by others. Maintain your composure.

Two Examples with Scenarios

Many excellent samples of written testimony can be found on the websites of respected nonprofit advocacy organizations, public policy institutes, and some government agencies. For example, see the following:

- Human Rights Watch http://www.hrw.org/en/search/apachesolr_search/congressional+testimony
- Cato Institute http://www.cato.org/pubs/pubs.html
- U.S. Government Accountability Office Reports and Testimonies http://www.gao.gov

Presented below are two examples of testimony written by the professional in a federal government workplace shown previously (chapter 3, Examples 1 and 2; chapter 6, Example 3) and by the citizen participating in local government shown previously (chapter 7). Scenarios introduce the context of each example.

Example 1.

Scenario

The Office of the Chief Surgeon, Reserve Armed Forces, is asked by interested congressional offices to justify the request for increased healthcare benefits for Reserve Component Soldiers. The House Armed Services Committee asks for a witness to testify in an upcoming hearing, specifically to justify increased dental care benefits. Senior officers are unavailable to write the testimony. The Chief of Patient Information is asked to draft a statement making the case for more dental care. A senior officer will orally deliver the testimony as witness. Delegation of writing or "ghost-writing" is characteristic in her workplace, as in others. The work of many professionals may be present, unidentified, in a document that carries only the organization's name and perhaps the name of the head administrator.

This action officer has not previously written congressional testimony. She is uncertain about the genre. Also, she does not know the committee's political agenda and related purpose for this hearing. She has little experience in writing for congressional audiences. She has not attended a hearing. There are no guidelines for writing congressional testimony and there is no template for a witness statement in the Army manual of procedure or style. As an astute professional communicator, however, she knows that context or genre, purpose, and audience are as important as message. So, despite a hectic schedule, she makes the time to prepare for writing. She consults textbooks on policy writing and government writing. She searches the Internet for samples of testimony by government witnesses. Reading actual samples gives her a feel for the expected form. Asking experienced peers about the committee gives her a sense of the context. She drafts a statement, and circulates it in her office for specialist review of content. She also sends it to a friend in another office, an experienced staff member for a senator who serves on relevant committees. The friend provides informal contextual review. Once formal review by staff is completed, the document comes back to the action officer. She makes all changes, then she gives the document to the senior officer who will be the witness. He reviews and requests changes, which she makes. She briefs the witness on the testimony's topic. Before the committee hearing date, a "mock" hearing will be held involving key participants from all agencies who reviewed the statement.

Unclassified
Statement by Colonel Michael Flynn
Chief Surgeon of the Reserve Armed Forces of America
Before the House Armed Services Committee
Subcommittee on Oversight and Investigation
Second Session, 110th Congress
on
Dental Readiness in the Reserve Armed Forces of America

May 17, 2008

Chairman Smith, Ranking Member Clay, as the Chief Surgeon of the Reserve Armed Forces of America, I am here today to answer your concerns about the dental readiness of the Soldiers in the Reserve Armed Forces of America.

The interest of the subcommittee on this issue is well placed. Dental readiness of our Citizen-Soldiers is a critical element in their capability to meet Department of Defense requirements for deployment.

Current Situation

The transition from a Strategic Reserve to an Operational Force has placed tremendous strain on the Reserve Armed Forces of America. Historically, as a strategic reserve, Soldiers and leaders of the Reserve Armed Forces addressed dental readiness issues at the mobilization station. The implementation of the Department of Defense's twelve month mobilization policy in February 2007 forced units to address dental readiness at home station in order to maximize collective training at the mobilization station.

The Reserve Armed Forces Medical Team, in conjunction with our Armed Forces Dental Command partners, has successfully managed this transition to an Operational Force. Since the beginning of the fiscal year, our units have prepared seven Brigade Combat Units (BCUs) for deployment, with each unit sending their units to the mobilization station over 90% dentally ready. These incredible readiness rates are a tremendous improvement over their previous mobilizations in 2003, when the average dental readiness rate was 13%. This significant decrease in the number of training days lost to dental treatment at mobilization station has enabled commanders to focus on collective training and maximize boots-on-ground time in theater.

Due to the low level of baseline dental readiness in the Reserve Armed Forces—currently only 40% of the force is dentally ready to deploy—truly herculean efforts must be applied by our units once a unit is alerted. Dental activities compete for the time of leaders, Soldiers, and families as a unit prepares to go to war. Soldiers that are cross-leveled to a ready unit dilute that unit's readiness and lengthen training timelines.

In order to improve the baseline readiness of the Reserve Armed Forces, the same programs, policies, and procedures that have been used to successfully prepare these BCUs need to be applied to our force as a whole.

Actions Taken

The Reserve Armed Forces, in conjunction with the Office of the Surgeon General and the Armed Forces Dental Command, has developed a multifaceted plan that has been approved by both the Army and Reserve Armed Forces leadership.

The cornerstone of this plan is the ability to provide dental treatment to our Soldiers outside of alert. [Additional content omitted.]

The Armed Forces Selected Reserve Dental Readiness Program (SRDRP) will enable units to provide dental treatment to soldiers through local contracts or utilizing the Reserve Health Readiness Program (RHRP).

The Reserve Armed Forces is a true reflection of our nation, and very few of our Citizen-Soldiers have private dental insurance. The participation rate in the TRICARE Reserve Dental Program has hit a plateau at 8%. The ability to provide treatment to our soldiers through the Armed Forces Selected Reserve Dental Readiness Program will have a tremendous impact on the readiness of the Reserve Armed Forces.

This program will also enable the Reserve Armed Forces to maximize the benefits of the Armed Forces Dental Command's initiatives. [Additional content omitted.]

With treatment programs in place, we must also address barriers to compliance with readiness requirements. Active component soldiers do not take unpaid leave to go to the dentist, nor should a Reserve Armed Forces soldier. The ability to provide two medical readiness days per soldier would be a powerful incentive for the soldier to complete readiness requirements, as well as a tool for our commanders to ensure compliance. [Additional content omitted.]

In addition to treatment and incentives, there must be enforcement as recommended by the Commission on Reserve Affairs. As alerted units prepare to go overseas, dental readiness is consistently the main reason for soldier ineligibility for deployment. The Armed Forces have multiple systems which provide unit and senior leaders the capability to track a unit's progress as they prepare for deployment...These tools must be applied and dental readiness enforced by leaders at all levels throughout the Reserve Armed Forces to improve the readiness of our soldiers.

Lastly, in order to execute these programs and sustain an increase in the dental readiness of the Reserve Armed Forces, we must have the appropriate staffing. The Reserve Armed Forces dental corps is currently less than 70% strength, and the majority of remaining providers are eligible for retirement. This committee is considering the Department of Defense's request to increase the retirement age of Reserve Armed Forces healthcare providers from age 65 to age 69. This would create the same standard for all three components of service. I would ask that this committee support that request and make that adjustment to the law. [Additional content omitted.]

Likewise, as a reserve component consisting largely of part-time warriors, the Reserve Armed Forces relies heavily on its cadre of full-time personnel to do the administration, maintenance, and training preparation required to produce a ready force. The president's budget request currently before Congress seeks an increase in the level of full-time manning in our force. This is critical. We urge Congress to support this increase.

Conclusion

This is a very exciting time to be in the Reserve Armed Forces. We have deployed over 300,000 dentally ready soldiers in support of the nation since September 11th 2001. Even so, we can do better. The Army and the Reserve Armed Forces are committed to our Citizen-Soldiers, by caring for them and improving their dental readiness.

I am grateful for this opportunity to appear before this subcommittee and look forward to answering your questions.

What this example shows. The testimony writer's consideration of semantics, or word meanings, is noteworthy. Sensitivity to politics surrounding Reserve Armed Forces healthcare in general, and dental care in particular, is shown here by careful word choice, such as "dental readiness" and "successfully managed transition" and "tremendous improvement." These wordings characterize achievement under difficult working conditions. Careful choice of organization is also evident. The testimony is organized narratively to tell a story of good management in a trying situation. These presentation techniques, deliberate word choice and storytelling, are not deceptive. They are not "spin." Rather, they are ethical (accurate, demonstrable) and rhetorically effective (credible) ways to characterize the organization's definition of the problem and message. Implicit meaning supports explicit statement well. The example illustrates an aspect of policy writing not noted in previous commentary on other samples, care for the meaningful interpretation of policy information. The language used to characterize a problem influences (Bardach 2005). A story about the problem informs (Stone 2002).

Example 2.

Scenario

A resident of a rural area known for the high quality of its cold-water fishing streams serves as a board member of a local conservation group. She learns of proposed changes in state policy for classifying waterways according to their quality. Four regional field hearings will be held to hear public comment on the agency's draft of a revised guidance manual for implementation of state water-quality regulations.

With the help of the state agency's staff, the resident obtains copies of the old and the new guidance manual, and she carefully reads the proposed changes. In her judgment, the new guidance draft weakens the standards. She alerts the local conservation group for which she is a board member. She asks the board to authorize her as spokesperson for the group in the upcoming hearings, and they do so. She writes testimony stating the position. She telephones the agency staff and asks to testify. In the call, she provides her credentials and says whom she represents. The staff member who is organizing the field hearings puts her on the schedule of witnesses.

In the hearing, she testifies with other witnesses from throughout her region. All witnesses provide a written copy of their testimony for the public record of the hearing. Following the testimonies, witnesses are encouraged to question the agency's managers. This reverses the usual question-and-answer procedure. Normally, conveners of a hearing question the witnesses. On this occasion, however, the agency managers want to demonstrate more than usual responsiveness to public comment.

Shown here is the written statement for the record (edited to reduce length). An oral summary was delivered.

Living with Exceptional Value

Testimony by the Penns Valley Conservation Association (PVCA)
http://www.pennsvalley.net

Public Hearing on Anti-Degradation Implementation Pennsylvania Department of Environmental Protection (PA-DEP) Bureau of Water Quality and Wastewater Management, Harrisburg, PA, August 1, 2001.

Thank you for providing us the opportunity to comment on DEP's draft Guidance for water quality protection. We strongly support DEP's anti-degradation program. Because we support it, we are concerned about how local communities such as ours perceive and participate in the program. We focus our testimony on the need to make implementation more inclusive and to ensure public participation. We offer related suggestions for revising the draft Guidance.

Our message to DEP is this: The goal of regulation is water quality protection. To the extent possible under Pennsylvania law, DEP's guidance should assume that implementation requires equal participation by petitioners or applicants and by communities that must live with the consequences of permitted or approved activity. The Department's function is to arbitrate between these parties and their interests while protecting the larger public interest. Petitioners and applicants are well prepared to present their legitimate interests and the commercial value of granting their request. Communities are less prepared to protect their interests. To carry out its function, DEP must ensure effective public participation.

Addressing those concerns one at a time, and relating them to the draft Guidance:

- *The goal of the program is water quality protection.* The draft Guidance does not make sufficiently clear that the purpose of the anti-degradation program is to ***protect*** all surface waters from adverse impacts on fish species, flora, and fauna by activities receiving a DEP permit or approval. True, policy is stated in chapter 1 and regulations as well as standards are identified at the start of chapter 2. But discussion sections throughout the draft create doubt that DEP will protect Pennsylvania's resources as required by regulation and federal law. [Additional content omitted.]

- *Guidance should assume that protection requires full participation of affected communities in addition to applicants or petitioners. DEP's function is to arbitrate between those interests and to protect the larger public interest.* The draft Guidance focuses exclusively on DEP's response to applicants or petitioners for permits or approvals. Community representatives

such as citizens' groups must also be recognized as key participants in permitting or approval processes. The public will refer
to the Guidance for policies, definitions, and procedures. The
Guidance might function as the procedures manual for public
participation, but the current draft does not serve that function
well. [Additional content omitted.]

- *To carry out its function, DEP needs effective public participation.* According to the Guidance, applicants or petitioners are
  encouraged to go beyond public notification to seek public
  input. That is not enough. The Department itself should actively
  seek and inform community input. On that topic, we must caution DEP about an effort, noted in chapter 4, on the processing of petitions, evaluations, and assessments to change a
  designated use. We are concerned about the pilot program of
  notifying landowners who border streams or stream segments
  being considered for HQ or EV status. That notification is dangerously insufficient. To notify landowners alone—and not local
  conservation groups, watershed associations, or municipal planning commissions—favors one constituency, property owners.
  Worse, to notify landowners without spelling out which activities
  or permits might affect a protected stream is likely to generate
  misinformed reaction. Backlash against protection is fueled by
  selective and cryptic public notification.

To summarize, experience teaches our organization that classifying
a stream as High Quality or Exceptional Value is relatively easy. But
implementation of protection on the ground in the community can be
hard. We've identified three main obstacles: public ignorance or misun-
derstanding of the anti-degradation program's purpose and methods,
burdensome permitting, and weak coordination among DEP bureaus
sharing responsibility for water quality protection.

I will briefly describe our experience in attempting to protect special
waters and a watershed. Direct practical experience is the context for
our testimony. [Additional content omitted.]

Conclusion
PVCA applauds the new ground the DEP is exploring in financing
watershed assessment and restoration activities by local communities through its Growing Greener program. Conservation groups like
the PVCA are adopting watershed-wide approaches to restoration,
while monitoring local activities for adverse effects on watersheds. We
would like to see watershed concepts reflected in DEP's regulatory

and permitting process. We would like support for comprehensive restoration efforts. And, we would like to see stronger intergovernmental coordination in protecting special waters.

This concludes our testimony. We refer you to our accompanying chapter-by-chapter list of suggested revisions to the draft Guidance. We are glad to answer questions now.

———————

What this example shows. This written statement is well organized to support spoken delivery under variable time limits. (Sometimes a witness is given more or less time than expected for presentation.) The introduction and summary can be presented in 1 minute. The introduction, summary, and list of concerns (without details beyond the first sentence in each section) can be presented in 2–3 minutes. The whole can be presented in 5–7 minutes (Task #1). However, individual sentences are too long for easy speaking and listening. Tighter sentence structure could make the statement easier to say and to hear.

Together, these examples illustrate the two halves of public hearing testimony. Example 1 on military dental readiness illustrates the oral summary, while Example 2 illustrates the written statement for the record. This combination serves the dual purposes of face-to-face discussion and on-the-record accountability.

Summary and Preview

Testimony in a public hearing is a highly visible way of getting your knowledge and perspective into the public record. Chapter 9, next, introduces an equally important, less visible way of influencing policy, providing public comment on proposed administrative action.

References

Bardach, E. 2005. Semantic Tips: A Summary, Appendix C. In *A practical guide for policy analysis: the eightfold path to more effective problem solving*. Congressional Quarterly Press.

Stone, D. 2002. Symbols. In *Policy paradox: the art of political decision making*, pp. 137–162. Rev. ed. New York: WW Norton.

CHAPTER 9

Written Public Comment: Influence Administration

Key Concept

- Public input on rule making

Too few people take advantage of an opportunity to set the standards and write the rules by which law is administered and enforced. When a government agency seeks public comment on proposed regulation, your response might make a difference. This chapter shows you how to write a formal public comment in rule making and adjudication procedures.

In federal government, after a law is enacted, an executive branch agency begins rule making to implement the law. This involves developing standards and regulations for administering and enforcing the law. As required by the Administrative Procedures Act as well as other laws and executive orders, the agency must seek public comment on the proposed standards and regulations before they can be put in force. Sometimes, oral hearings are held; typically, written comments are requested.

While federal agencies are required to seek public comment, they have discretion regarding the use of comments received. In federal and many states' rule making procedures, agencies may choose or choose not to describe whether and how they modified the proposed regulation in response to the comments received. For example, in the milk labeling case (chapter 1) the Pennsylvania Department of

Agriculture (PDA)'s Bureau of Food Safety and Laboratory Services described a modification this way:

> PDA has received a great deal of input on the standards set forth in [the new standard on milk labeling announced on October 24, 2007] and previously decided to inform you on November 21, 2007 that certain deadlines stated in that document were being changed from January 1, 2008 to February 1, 2008. We are now in a position to inform you further as to the results of reviewing the input we received. Enclosed please find a new document titled "Revised Standards and Procedures for the Approval of Proposed Labeling of Fluid Milk" dated January 17, 2008...Please review this document carefully and govern yourself accordingly.

In state and local governments, public comment is not sought as routinely as in federal government. However, states must seek public comment in regulatory procedures for granting, revoking, or renewing permits for activities that affect public life.

Regrettably, few citizens know about this opportunity to provide input, and few engage it. As a result, narrowly interested groups dominate the rule making process. Broader participation is needed.

Federal, state, and local agencies welcome any type of comment that can help them make and justify their decisions. The comment might be a technical analysis, a philosophical argument, an opinion based on personal experience, advocacy, or a request to hold a public meeting on the proposed action. Responsible agencies review all written comments. They take seriously well-prepared comments that suggest realistic and feasible alternatives.

Public comment is important because public policy broadly affects present and future life in society and ecosystems. A call for public comment invites any member of the public—individuals, communities, organizations—to influence the standards and regulations that affect real lives, livelihoods, and environments. Public comment is easy to make. Anybody can write a useful comment. The more who do so, the better the likelihood of good government.

How to Write a Public Comment

Goal: Knowledge of administrative procedures for implementing law, including the public's role in implementation.

Objective: To influence the administration of a law by contributing information relevant to standard setting, rule making, or permitting.

Product: Formal written comment.

Scope: Limited to the specific proposed administrative action.

Strategy: Base comments on your authority to respond, whether based on personal experience, organizational advocacy, vocational or professional background, or specialized knowledge.

While expert commentary is always appropriate, you need not be an expert to comment. Administrators want and need to hear from anyone who can make a useful comment. There is no template for public comments, unlike legal briefs. A simple letter can have an impact. If friends or a community organization shares your views, you might want to present a collective comment. You might sign for the group, or all individuals involved might sign, or the organization's officers might sign.

Task #1. Find calls for public comment

The U.S. government's official source for notifications of proposed rule making is the *Federal Register,* published daily. You can find the *Federal Register* either in government information depository libraries or online at http://www.gpoaccess.gov/fr.

You will find calls for comment in the section titled "Proposed Rules" or the section titled "Notices." Look for announcements by agencies authorized to act on topics of concern to you.

Alternatively, if you already know the executive branch department, and within it the relevant agency, that administers laws in your area of concern, do not go initially to the *Register.* It can be overwhelming, and you might have to look at the index every day to follow the government's activities on an issue of concern. Instead, first try the website of the relevant department (the Department of Transportation, for example); search there for the relevant agency (National Highway and Traffic Safety Administration, for example). If you do not know what department or agency to search for, go to the website of an advocacy group associated with your concern. Browsing there is likely to turn up the name of both the department and agency. Then proceed with searching the agency's website for notifications.

If you are concerned about a state issue, you can find calls for public comment in state notifications, such as the *Pennsylvania Bulletin* or the *New York State Register.* Every state has one.

Familiarize yourself with the index and other finding aids for the state publication you are likely to use often.

Alternatively, if you know the jurisdiction for your concern, go first to the website of the state agency with jurisdiction. Or go to the websites of interested associations and advocacy groups to find where you can make a comment on an active issue.

If you want to comment on a local government matter, consult local newspapers. Local government calls for public comment are published in the public notices section of newspapers. Notifications are also posted in local government offices or, possibly, on their websites.

Task #2. Write the public comment document

In most respects, writing a public comment is like writing any other policy document. The demands for preparation and planning are the same. The same criteria for clarity, credibility, and conciseness apply. One possible difference: some calls for public input specify the exact information needed. If the call to which you are responding does specify the contents, be sure to provide them as requested. If you have additional information, include it too, but not at the expense of requested contents.

To help ensure that your comment will be taken seriously, include the following features and qualities:

- Narrow focus
- Evidence, analyses, and references supporting your view
- Indication of public support of your view
- Positive and feasible alternatives

Before you write, use the Method (chapter 2) to plan. After you write, check the product against the expected standards (checklists, chapter 2).

Three Examples with Scenarios

Examples here show administrative policy making. Example 1 illustrates rule making by a federal agency, while Example 2 illustrates adjudicative procedure by a state agency. Comment by experts, by a nonprofit organization, and by a citizens group is shown. Scenarios provide context for each example.

Example 1.

Scenario

A national transportation safety investigative board holds four days of hearings on air bag safety. The board, which reports both to the Congress and to the executive branch, is concerned about the unanticipated high rates of injury from air bag deployment. The witness list for the hearings includes representatives of auto manufacturers, insurance companies, safety institutes, auto safety advocacy groups, air bag manufacturers, and auto parts suppliers. The purpose of the hearings is to enable the board to make recommendations for improving air bag safety.

Based on the board's ensuing recommendations and its own investigations, the National Highway Traffic Safety Administration (the federal agency responsible for automotive safety regulations) announces that it intends to modify the current standard for air bags. The agency announces its proposed modification in the *Federal Register* and calls for public comment.

In response, two experts in automotive safety jointly write a technical comment (Example 1, below, this chapter). They point out shortcomings in the agency's proposed modification, and they propose an alternative.

Later, in the preamble to their next published notice on air bag safety, the agency summarizes all comments received. It says how the comments influenced their plans to modify the standard. Here is an extract from that preamble: "In response to the public comments on our 1998 proposal and to other new information obtained since issuing the proposal, we are issuing a supplemental proposal that updates and refines the amendments under consideration." In an appendix, the agency stated its reasons for rejecting the experts' proposed alternative.

This written comment is a technical analysis written by professionals in the field of automotive safety and submitted in the rule making process described in the scenario.

Comment to The Docket Concerning Amendments to FMVSS 208, Occupant Crash Protection

Summary of Comments

Federal motor vehicle safety standards (FMVSS) must, by law, meet the need for motor vehicle safety. This proposal (Docket No. NHTSA 98–4405; Notice 1) purports to meet that need by requiring advanced air bags. In fact, it is primarily written to address the problem of inflation induced injuries and would provide little additional protection.

The worst of the inflation-induced injuries resulted in several hundred fatalities to children and out-of-position adults (including those sitting too close to the steering wheel) and from late, low-speed crash air bag deployments. NHTSA [National Highway Traffic Safety Administration] had assumed that manufacturers would conduct comprehensive air bag testing to ensure that inflation would not inflict injury under reasonable foreseeable conditions. It is arguable (although probably not practical policy) that NHTSA could address inflation-induced injuries under safety defect provisions of the National Traffic and Motor Vehicle Safety Act. [Additional content omitted.]

A key part of this notice proposes two options: (1) tests of air bag systems with dummies in close proximity to ensure that inflation induced injuries are unlikely, or (2) requirements for occupant sensors to ensure that air bags will not inflate if an occupant is in a position where he or she is at risk of injury from the inflating air bag.

In response to the proposed alternatives, we expect manufacturers to choose occupant sensors to prevent air bag inflation for certain occupant situations. This untested sensor technology might actually increase casualties because of inaccurate determinations of occupant risks and degraded reliability from the added complexity.

Experts in the field have suggested a number of potential air bag design and performance features that might reduce inflation induced injuries. The Canadian government and NHTSA deserve credit for their research and analysis in this field despite NHTSA's belated recognition that an official response was necessary. It is not clear which approach would be most effective, or even most cost-effective, but we think it is unlikely that NHTSA's proposed regulation will yield an optimal result.

This notice [of proposal amendments] also fails to address occupant protection challenges involving one to two orders of magnitude more casualties for which feasible technologies are available. These include raising safety belt use to near universality, protection of occupants in rollover crashes, and addressing compatibility problems between passenger cars and light trucks.

Many of these deficiencies can be overcome with a third alternative that retains the simplicity of the original automatic occupant crash protection standard; does not introduce complex, untested occupant sensors; and meets other needs for motor vehicle safety. It depends fundamentally on NHTSA's willingness to propose acceptable, effective inducements for using safety belts.

Problems with NHTSA's Proposal
[Additional content omitted.]

"Please Don't Eat the Daisies"
[An argument that the government should not have to tell manufacturers everything they should or should not do to protect people. Omitted here.]

A Third Option Would Encourage Belt Use
We are proposing that a third option be added to NHTSA's notice that would ensure safety belt use with acceptable and effective belt use inducements built into the vehicle. [Additional content omitted.]

NHTSA must recognize that the fundamental problem with its occupant restraint policy is that a substantial minority of motorists does not use safety belts. In fact, a much larger proportion of those most likely to be involved in serious crashes drive unbelted. Nearly universal belt use is critical to any rational occupant crash protection program.

Using the Marketplace
[An argument for useful safety consumer information. Omitted here.]

Diagnosing Problems and Evaluating Change
[Additional content omitted.]

Detailed Comments
[Additional content omitted.]

Background and Policy
[Additional content omitted.]

An Alternative to the Proposed Amendment
Our specific proposal is that NHTSA add a third option to its notice on advanced air bags. Under this option:

- A manufacturer must install an effective, but not onerous safety belt use inducement in a new motor vehicle of a type that would be permitted under the "interlock" amendment (15 U.S.C.1410b) to the National Traffic and Motor Vehicle Safety Act. [Additional content omitted.]

- A motor vehicle must meet comparative injury criteria of FMVSS 208 and in addition [in crashworthiness tests using dummies] there can be no contact between the head of the driver or passenger dummy and any part of the vehicle (other than the air bag or belt restraint system) or any other part of the dummy, in a frontal barrier crash at a speed of up to 35 mph with belted occupants. [Additional content omitted.]

- Air bags may not deploy under any frontal crash speed barrier impacts below 16 mph. [Additional content omitted.]

- Vehicles would be subject to an offset barrier test similar to that proposed in this notice. [Additional content omitted.]

Consumer Information and the Market for Safety
[Additional content omitted.]

Discussion
Our alternative would provide occupant crash protection that is at least equal in all respects to that provided by the present standard and NCAP consumer information program. [Additional content omitted.]

This proposal would substantially increase belt use and, because of the head impact requirements, would ensure that air bags provide good head protection. Air bags that can meet this criterion would provide some frontal crash protection to the small number of unbelted occupants (who would, of course, be unbelted by their own conscious choice).

If manufacturers would choose our alternative, it would save a minimum of 7000 lives per year compared with the present FMVSS208, making it one of the most cost-effective standards ever. (The full comment can be found at http://www.regulations.gov. See NHTSA 1999–6407-0073. It has as Appendix 1 a further petition on the subject.)

Example 2.

Scenario

A state environmental protection department's bureau of mining, which regulates mineral extraction industries in the state, announces a proposed revision in a mining company's operating permit. In accordance with "sunshine" requirements for permitting processes, the agency publishes the applicant's proposal to mine deeper than its original permit allowed. The mining company is asking the bureau to remove restrictions on the company's operation at a specific site. The primary restriction prohibits mining at levels that might adversely affect local groundwater quantity and quality. The restriction is warranted in a region where well-water supply varies according to groundwater conditions and where high quality cold-water trout fishing streams are fed by local springs near the mining site.

In response to the bureau's call for public comment on the mine operator's request for permit revision, a local environmental conservation group and a local civic organization write letters of comment (Examples 2 and 3, below, this chapter). Others including a national sport fishing group, local businesses dependent on tourism, and individual citizens write letters too. At the request of the civic organization, the agency holds a public meeting. The conservation group hires a professional stenographer (who is also a notary public) to transcribe the meeting. In addition, the group invites local news reporters. The meeting is well attended. The bureau officials, the mine operator, and the residents of the region affected by the mine vigorously discuss the request to lift restrictions on the mine. After the meeting, the conservation group provides the transcript to the bureau as a written record of public comment. If administrative litigation regarding this permit ensues, the transcript will provide evidence.

In announcing its decision later, the agency says, "The many public comments the Department received regarding this application formed the basis for modifications to the permit revision

> and resulted in changes in [the mining company's] proposed min-
> ing plan." The bureau's decision is to allow deeper mining, but to
> require new modifications in the mining plan intended to protect
> groundwater conditions.

An attorney member of the local environmental conservation group,
in collaboration with members expert in hydrogeologyand water
quality engineering, wrote this technical analysis to comment on a
mining permit application. The chair of the group's relevant committee signed and submitted the comment.

TECHNICAL ANALYSIS

July 29, 2001

Michael W. Smith
District Mining Manager
Pennsylvania Department of Environmental Protection
P.O. Box 209 Hawk Run, PA 16840-0209
VIA Hand Delivery

Re: Con-Stone, Inc's, June 7, 2001, application to revise permit
#14920301

Dear Mr. Smith

The Penns Valley Conservation Association (PVCA) has reviewed
Con-Stone, Inc.'s, June 7, 2001, application to revise permit
#14920301 to allow removal of the Valentine Limestone below the
1080' elevation. PVCA wishes to work cooperatively with Con-Stone
and the Pennsylvania Department of Environmental Protection
(DEP) to ensure that mining operations protect the watershed surrounding the Aaronsburg Operation, including Elk and Pine Creeks

[state-designated Exceptional Value (EV) stream] and Penns Creek [state-designated High-Quality (HQ) stream]. In that spirit of cooperation, and for protection of those streams, PVCA requests denial of Con-Stone's current application for the following reasons.

1. PVCA recommends retaining special conditions 1, 2, and 4 in Part B, Noncoal Surface Mining Permit No 14920301, Revised July 13, 1999, Special Conditions or Requirements. As District Mining Manager Michael W. Smith said in an August 27, 1999, letter to Con-Stone, "The mining limit of 1080 feet was originally established to keep mining activity out of the average seasonal low water table to minimize the potential for impacts to groundwater and to Spring S-26. We are not convinced that mining below 1080 feet can be accomplished without added risk of water impact." [Additional content omitted.]

2. To manage the risks of mining below the water table, the proposed amendment calls for phased mining with a progressively deeper penetration of the water table. However, there is a total lack of detail in the permit amendment regarding the specific steps to be taken in the phased mining process. There should be clear language in the permit that stipulates consecutive mining and reclamation and attaches some time schedule and methodology for data analysis and reporting prior to advancing to the next phase of mining.

3. In PVCA's original discussions with DEP, Mike Smith indicated that Con-Stone would have to develop a new infiltration basin system to dispose of the groundwater pumped from the quarry. The permit amendment is contrary to this position as it utilizes the infiltration galleries currently designated for storm water disposal. PVCA requests that separate infiltration systems covered by separate NPDES permits be developed for the storm water and groundwater pumped from the pit.

4. The materials contained in the permit amendment do not adequately describe the hydrogeologic conditions. An appropriately scaled map showing the current pit location, the water table configuration, the location of all boreholes, the sedimentation basin, and infiltration galleries should be prepared. Without water table contour mapping, it is impossible

to address issues such as recirculation of the water pumped from the mine. [Additional content omitted.]

5. The May 7–10, 2001, pit pumping test performed by the mine operator provides little useful information regarding the extent of [potential loss of water supply] due to mining operations. [Additional content omitted.] If DEP is going to grant the requested amendment, PVCA requests a special condition that Con-Stone is responsible for replacing the water supply for any water losses that result from mining operations.

6. The McWhorter Model used to estimate the volume of groundwater to be intercepted during mining is extremely simplistic. It does not reflect a state of the art effort. In the context of the EV protection of the watershed, a much more comprehensive modeling effort is warranted. "Ideal aquifer" calculations such as those used to calculate inflow to the pit are not applicable in this setting. [Additional content omitted.]

7. The permit amendment submission does not address the continuous turbidity monitors currently maintained at Spring 26 and Pine Creek just upstream of Spring 26. The continuous turbidity monitoring should be continued, the costs associated with the monitoring should be borne by Con-Stone, and the data collection system discussed at the December 15, 2000, meeting with DEP should be implemented. [Additional content omitted.] In addition, monitoring should be expanded, again at Con-Stone's cost, to be more complete by including all biological and chemical monitoring required by DEP's water quality anti-degradation regulations and implementation guidelines.

8. The mining permit amendment does not address the issue of the potential for fines (fine-grained debris) contained in the backfill to be mobilized into the groundwater system during surface water runoff events or during high water table conditions. [Additional content omitted.] A detailed assessment of the potential for significant contamination of conduit flow system from the fines contained within the backfill should be performed.

9. The mining permit amendment says that "if continuous flow rates greater than 475 GPM are experienced, then further

extractions within that area below the water table will not occur unless drought conditions result in an additional decline of the groundwater table." This statement should be revised to specify what "additional decline" is necessary to allow mining operations to resume.

10. The permit amendment submission does not appear to be signed and sealed by a licensed professional geologist.

11. PVCA believes Con-Stone must apply for a new or revised NPDES [National Pollution Discharge] permit for the proposed quarry dewatering activities.

12. If DEP is going to allow any mining below 1080 feet, PVCA requests that the special conditions 3 and 5–21 in Part B, Non-coal Surface Mining Permit No. 14920301, Revised July 13, 1999, Special Conditions or Requirements continue to apply to all mining operations at the Aaronsburg Operation.

13. PVCA does not believe that Con-Stone has complied with all necessary pre-permit requirements under DEP's water quality anti-degradation regulations and implementation guidelines. [Additional content omitted.] Further, the application has not sought review by local and county governments to ensure compatibility with applicable regulations, ordinances, and comprehensive plans and to allow government to identify local and regional environmental and economic issues that should be considered.

Sincerely,
J. Thomas Doman Chair,
Watershed Committee Member,
Board of Directors, PVCA

cc: Jeff Confer, Con-Stone, Inc.
Hon. Jake Corman, Pennsylvania Senate
Hon. Kerry Benninghoff, Pennsylvania
House of Representatives
Pennsylvania Trout Unlimited

Example 3.

This is a letter by a citizens group requesting the public meeting described in the scenario, above.

CITIZEN GROUP'S LETTER

July 16, 2001

Re: Application for amendment for Con-Stone mining permit #14920301, Aaronsburg Operation

District Mining Manager
Department of Environmental Protection
Bureau of Mining
Hawk Run District Office
PO Box 209 Hawk Run, PA 16840-0209

On behalf of the Aaronsburg Civic Club I am requesting a public conference on the proposed amendment to the above permit. Again this year, we are offering our facility, the Aaronsburg Civic Club Community Building, for that purpose. As you are aware last year's public meeting was well attended and provided an opportunity for residents to state their concerns and for Con-Stone and DEP to address them. This is as it should be in a free and democratic society.

I strongly urge you to hold a public meeting on the latest proposed permit revisions. Two concerns that have been brought to my attention are (1) the potential degradation of underground and surface water, and (2) mining on land previously designated for storage.
Please contact me to reserve our facility.

Sincerely yours,
Earl Weaver, President
Aaronsburg Civic Club

What these examples show. All three examples exhibit qualities of effective public policy communication (checklists, chapter 2) and authoritative argument (chapter 5).

Example 1 on auto safety and Example 2 on stream water quality show evidence of public support for their claims not by opinion polls, but rather by invoking federal motor vehicle safety standards and state environmental protection regulations. Example 3 invokes the authority of "sunshine" mandates for public participation in a government decision about activity affecting their town.

Examples 1 and 2 are detailed and technical. Although the contents are organized and subheadings are provided to aid comprehension, some of the details (test results, for example) might be moved to an appendix. However, the choice to use that option should depend on the writer's knowledge of the circumstances in which the documents will be read and used. As noted in the commentary on earlier examples, writers should be certain that all readers can access the entire document before deciding to move crucial details to an appendix.

Taken together, the three examples suggest the robust potential of the genre, formal public comment, for getting concerns on the public agenda and in the public record.

Summary and Preview

It is surprising that few of us comment on action that government intends to take when the responsible agencies directly ask us to do so. This chapter aims to encourage and enable the practice of publicly commenting. Democratic self-governance depends on our willingness to intervene in the process. Concluding remarks, next, point to ways the Internet is increasing our capacity for intervention.

Conclusion:
Continuity and Change

Key Concepts

- Continuity
- Change
- Networked writing

Whenever public policy is made, communication will continue to be necessary and integral. Purposes will persist while processes will change. New communication media will emerge.

Genres introduced in this guide—defining policy problems, researching legislative history, arguing, petitioning, proposing, briefing, testifying, and commenting on proposed action—will continue, perhaps in altered forms. Cultural expectations will continue to value usefulness, clarity, credibility, and authority. In short, policy writers will continue to face demands for understanding the cultural context of policy making, and for applying their understanding and knowledge to communicate purposefully and ethically in the process.

What changes might you anticipate? Developments in communication technology will bring the greatest change. Recently, the Internet has emerged as an all-inclusive medium or the medium on which any information can be delivered to users. Owing to new network capabilities, information is no longer tied to a particular communication device. Content's form is no longer determined by its medium of delivery. For example, a telephone conversation does not require a telephone; the conversation might be conducted via the Internet. Similarly, radio or television broadcasts do not require a radio or television, and print documents do not require paper. Information created originally in any of those media may now be adaptively communicated, received, and used on the Internet through the World Wide Web interface. Or, information may originate and function entirely in the Internet environment.

What does the inclusive or all-media Internet mean for policy writers? The immediate, practical answer is that communicators must now choose how to use the Internet for their purposes. The choice is not whether to use the network, but how to use it.

To reflect more generally on the question, assume a framework of mixed continuity and change. As continuity, recall that people in policy making roles will go on communicating in forms associated with their institution- or process-related roles (chapter 2). As change, reflect on recent historical changes of infrastructure that enabled new ways of communicating. For example, cellular wireless technology changed telephone use; now cell phones are changing computer use (Markoff 2009). In that frame of mixed continuity and change, bring the policy process into focus. Recall (from chapter 2) three categories of policy role-players: professionals inside government, professionals outside government, and active citizens.

Professionals who create and use information inside government will increasingly perform work via e-government, which means conducting jurisdictional responsibilities online (*Wikipedia, the free encyclopedia*). Claimed benefits of e-government include better interoperability among agencies and greater transparency between government and citizens. Evidence suggests that the transparency benefit is real. In the United States, Internet users routinely access governmental information online rather than by other means. In 2003, the Pew Internet & American Life study reported "77% of American Internet users went online to search for information from government agencies or to communicate with them" (Allison and Williams 2008). Thus, professionals in government agencies now routinely provide information and interact with information users through websites. The sites are expected to meet prescribed standards for the electronic exchange of information (American National Standards Institute and the National Institute of Standards and Technology), as well as traditional standards for usefulness, clarity, credibility, and authority.

Beyond informing and interacting with the public, professionals in government and elected officeholders apply the Internet's capabilities to policy making functions, too. Problem definition and policy analysis are examples. Sound, visualization, animation, and statistical modeling in "decision theaters" of integrative technologies enhance the representations of conditions, problems, and proposed solutions (Arizona State University Decision Theater).

For professionals outside government, the Internet provides new tools for creating knowledge to be used in policy design. Such tools include searchable databases, content management systems, and subscriber-only discussion groups that link to government websites. Experts use these tools collaboratively to draft reports for government use. For example, multinational teams of scientists now routinely collaborate on reports about climate change to inform governments globally. Nongovernmental institutions created specifically for this purpose include a treaty, the United Nations Framework Convention on Climate Change (UNFCCC) and a working group created jointly by the World Meteorological Organization and the United Nations, the Intergovernmental Panel on Climate Change (IPCC).

The Internet may hold the most potential for active citizens. The all-inclusive communication medium builds capacity for participation and intervention in governance. For example, Barack Obama's 2008 presidential campaign showed that the electorate could organize as a mega-interest group through Internet capabilities for email, text messaging, blogging, and social networking. Internet-enabled coalitions challenge the conventional wisdom that dispersed populations and single individuals cannot influence the policy process. Dairy farmers scattered across Pennsylvania who organized rapidly into groups via email to achieve policy change (chapter 1) illustrate the power of networked individuals. Additionally, the Internet greatly expands the single individual's capacity to be informed about governance. If Google News can now search 4,500 global news sources continuously and deliver summaries personalized according to your zip code or your browsing pattern, might it someday search global government records databases and deliver multinational legislative histories on specified topics at your request?

Limits on change should be acknowledged. Cultural context, especially Internet access, is a limit. Geopolitical, economic, and infrastructure constraints determine who has Internet access. Now, access is not universal or evenly distributed. Latest statistics on Internet usage penetration in populations by world region show that penetration in North American regions is 73.6 percent, as compared with 17.0 percent worldwide and 5.3 percent in African regions, for example (Internet World Stats Usage and Population Statistics). In developed nations, such as the United States, rural locales have uneven access or no access. It remains to be seen whether e-government will serve everyone equally well.

Summary and Looking Forward

Public policy writers can look forward to continuity and to change, especially Internet-related change. As student, intern, professional, officeholder, or citizen, you might wish or you might be required to write in adapted or new Internet forms. When that happens, start by consulting the appendices that follow next, here. There you will find this guide's principles (know-how) applied to networked communication along with resources for skill development (how-to).

References

Allison, L., and M. F. Williams. 2008. *Writing for the government.* New York: Pearson Longman.

American National Standards Institute (ANSI). http://www.ansi.org. Accessed 18 December, 2008.

Arizona State University Decision Theater. http://decisiontheater.org. Accessed 18 December, 2008.

"e-Government." *Wikipedia, the free encyclopedia.* http://en.wikipedia.org/wiki/E-Government. Accessed 18 December, 2008.

Intergovernmental Panel on Climate Change (IPCC). http://www.ipcc.ch/about/index.htm. Accessed 18 December, 2008.

Internet World Stats Usage and Population Statistics. http://www.internetworldstats.com/stats.htm. Accessed 18 December, 2008.

Markoff, J. *The cellphone, navigating our lives.* NYTimes.com. 17 February, 2009.

National Institute of Standards and Technology (NIST). http://www.nist.
gov. Accessed December 18, 2008.

United Nations Framework Convention on Climate Change. http://
unfccc.int/essential_background/convention/items/2627.php. Accessed
December 18, 2008.

Public Policy Writing for the Web

Key Concept

- Adapting public policy information to the Web

In the 1980s with the gradual uptake of email, chat, file or document transfer, and other text-processing applications, the Internet network became a means of everyday communication. In the mid-1990s the information-processing application World Wide Web pushed the Internet into the background where it became infrastructure. The popular Web interface, in effect, became the network. A new genre, the website emerged to frame developments in online communication. Multimedia, connectivity, and interactivity became norms for content. In the early 2000s, integrated media and social networking again changed the norms for content, while cellular telephone technology widened network access. The practical lesson to draw from this history? Web-writing techniques change in tandem with an evolving communication technology and expanding global network. The best practice is to continue learning.

This appendix can help you intelligently adapt the craft of public policy writing to Web conditions. Email was previously discussed (chapter 7). Here, the public policy website is the focus. Emphasis is on writing clear text for sites. This appendix informs know-how by offering heuristics or conceptual tools for presenting public policy information on the Web. Resources for skill development in specific Web-writing practices are identified.

Case

The Employee Free Choice Act, also known as the Card Check Bill, was passed by the House but not voted on in the Senate in 2008. It was reintroduced in 2009

> to amend the National Labor Relations Act to establish an efficient system to enable employees to form, join, or assist labor organizations, to provide for mandatory injunctions for unfair labor practices during organizing efforts, and for other purposes (H.R.1409 and S. 560).

Big labor unions including the American Federation of Labor and Congress of Industrial Organizations (AFL-CIO), a voluntary federation of 56 national and international labor unions, pushed Congress to approve the legislation. The U.S. Chamber of Commerce, a federation representing 3 million businesses as well as state and local chambers, industry associations in the United States, and 112 American chambers in other countries, pushed Congress to oppose it.

The AFL-CIO (http://www.aflcio.org) and the U.S. Chamber (http://www.uschamber.com) used their websites for activism to create awareness and mobilize action. In activist terms, creation of awareness means communicating an interest in a problem or a position regarding it intentionally to persuade others to share the interest or agree with the position. Mobilization means organizing interested people to act or react to influence public policy.

In this case, the AFL-CIO and U.S. Chamber aggregated representations of the subject and capabilities for expressing opinion on their websites. Options included

- email for action alerts or announcements calling on interested people to contact Congress members and newspaper editors using content provided in the alert ("canned" letters to legislators and "astroturf" to editors);
- podcasts or prerecorded audio material;
- videos or prerecorded multimedia material;
- blogs, shared online journals maintained by individuals or organizations for public posting;
- wikis or collections of web pages to which anyone with access can contribute or modify content.

While debate continued, people interested in knowing the AFL-CIO's or the U.S. Chamber's position on the Employee Free Choice Act or in joining their advocacy could do so through links to these options on their websites. After debate and action, the content might or might not be accessible in archives linked to the website. That public record depends on voluntary organizational policies for retaining content.

What this case shows. The Web now serves as one of many competing platforms where policy agendas are enacted and policy work is conducted. The Web offers advantages of transmission speed, information delivery to local and global users, low publishing costs, and 24-hour access. In this case, the purpose was advocacy.

More broadly, this case illustrates now-common practices of integrating many communication options with websites, not only for advocacy purposes. Other nonprofit organizational and governmental websites show other purposes. Examples include

- documentation of policy analysis by publishing briefs and full texts of reports (The Cato Institute at http://www.cato.org and The Brookings Institution at http://www.brookings.org);
- performance of administrative rule making by managing electronic submission of comments (http://regulations.gov);
- public engagement by civic discussion forums (http://e-democracy.org).

Across the spectrum of policy work settings, writers need to learn practices of creating textual content for websites.

The Web alters writing practice, but it does not invalidate the standards for writing in the cultural context. Features of Web content must accommodate normative qualities of public policy information. For effectiveness, a Web communication must fit the culture of public policy making. Like much else in policy making, the fit might be messy. You are reintroduced to cultural expectations previously discussed (checklists, chapter 2) and offered resources for thoughtfully adapting them to Web-writing conditions, below.

Public Policy Communication Addresses a Specific Audience about a Specific Problem

The touchstones for communicating with actors in a policy process are your definition of a problem relative to others and your role relative to other actors' roles (chapter 3). Choices about Web use start with those touchstones. The complexity of public policy audiences, which involve multiple interests and diverse role players, calls for special consideration in content creation. Here's a good general principle for public policy Web communicators to follow: assume that Web communication is one-to-many, and learn all you can about your actual and potential audience(s).

Generally, Web-writing guides do not offer methods of complexity management and multidimensional audience analysis that are sufficient to meet the demands of public policy writing. A notable exception is the chapter on government websites in the specialized guide *Writing for the Government* (Allison and Williams 2008). If you are a government writer, another helpful source is Webcontent.gov's "Knowing Your Audience and Doing Market Research" (http://www. usa.gov/webcontent/improving/evaluating/audience.shtml).

Conceptually, try this heuristic for thinking about one-to-many public policy communication on the Web. Imagine a website as a public space, perhaps a forum, a marketplace, or a commons. The space contains objects or bits of varied kinds of stuff. In this public space, people are freely coming and going, noticing some objects but not noticing others, pausing to consider an object or hurrying past it, putting stuff in and taking stuff out of baskets, and so forth. Imagine the people as actors or role players in the policy process of concern to you. The objects are bits of your intended content.

Look closer at the scene. What's happening? What types of actors or role players are present? Why are they here? Who's doing what? What abilities do they have? Do all have the same abilities? Which actors are putting bits in their baskets? Which bits? What do you want the actors to do with the bits?

When you know your purpose, whether it is advocacy, analysis, public engagement, or another intention, conceive your audience(s) to anticipate their need(s), purpose(s), and actions of engaging the content. Narrative and dramatic imagination aids the practice of information design for Web users. Information design is the skill of preparing information so that people can use it efficiently and effectively.

To translate this scene to an information design for a public policy website, work from the assumptions that

- a site has multiple users who have diverse purposes;
- a site has multiple components of content expressed in varied information types;
- components are organized into a site index or map of content for multiple users and diverse purposes;
- a site has multiple functions;
- functions are anticipated in a site navigation plan;
- a site is planned as a whole before individual components are planned;
- individual components are "chunked" or constructed with a focus local to that component;
- individual components are explicitly labeled or captioned;
- a site as a whole and individual components meet standards for usability including clarity and accessibility (discussed in more detail below).

Public Policy Communication Has a Purpose Related to a Specific Policy Action

Each action in a policy cycle (Figure 1.1, chapter 1) requires information created by both governmental and nongovernmental actors (cultural context, chapter 2). For policy professionals in U.S. federal government, the institutional workplace significantly influences choices about Web use. Executive branch departments and agencies use the network extensively for informing and interacting with the public and for administrative functions. Presently, e-government (conclusion) is practiced mostly by administrative departments, agencies, and offices of the executive branch. The legislative and judicial branches use the Web for fewer purposes. Congressional and Supreme Court offices use the Web primarily for public information and access to public records.

In government settings, accountability demands that a communication have an identifiable purpose that is disclosed. Nonprofit organizations and individual citizens have more latitude. For these actors, public disclosure and other aspects of accountability might be voluntary rather than obligatory. Writers who want more information on voluntary self-regulation might consult the guidance on public disclosure in "Principles for Good Governance and Ethical Practice" developed by Independent Sector, a nonpartisan coalition of nonprofit organizations (http://www.independentsector.org/panel/main.htm).

Public Policy Communication Represents Authority Accurately

Credible policy communications identify their role in the policy process. Role identification shows the kind of power the communication represents. Roles may be evident in the presenting individual's or group's title (for example, Senator X or Office of the Governor) or by reference in the content (for example, Jane Y and other union members).

Also, a document's origination and, if appropriate, the writers' names should be identified. Contact information must be provided. These attributions give credibility because they enable verification. Writers who want to know more about credibility in Web communications might consult the research-based "Stanford Guidelines for Web Credibility" (http://credibility.stanford.edu/guidelines) developed by Stanford University's Persuasive Technology Lab (http://captology.stanford.edu).

Public Policy Communications Use Appropriate Form and Content

Appropriateness of form starts with the writer's choice of a genre (Method, chapter 2). Genre choices in the Web environment require careful thought. As the case of AFL-CIO and U.S. Chamber of Commerce communication discussed earlier in this chapter shows, websites now creatively meld many communication functions and forms. Caution should accompany creativity, however. Options might be wasted if users cannot access them. Accessibility is discussed later in this appendix.

Appropriate content choices start with the writer's purpose and the audience's purpose (Method, chapter 2). In the cultural context, rights and responsibilities are associated with information's creation and use. Generally, for nongovernmental policy actors in the United States, information is expression and free speech is a right with legal constraints. As illustration, see commentary on "Free Speech Rights of Nonprofits" on the watchdog group OMBWatch's website (http://ombwatch.org). For actors in government, information is a public trust. More stringent legal constraints apply to government sources than to others. For illustration by one federal government executive department, see the U.S. Department of Agriculture's "Policies and Links," "FOIA" (Freedom of Information Act), and "Information Quality" in small print at the bottom of the department website's homepage (http://www.usda.gov/wps/portal/usdahome).

Writers who want to learn more about information rights and responsibilities in democracy, particularly about the freedom of information, might consult "Federal Open Government Guide" (http://www.rcfp.org/fogg) developed by the advocacy group The Reporters' Committee for Freedom of the Press (http://www.rcfp.org/foia).

Public Policy Communication Is Designed for Use

Policy information is expected to be useful. In the cultural context of policy making, that means content that is relevant for a purpose and accountable (Method, chapter 2). Content is also expected to meet usability standards for public information including clarity and accessibility.

Clarity is associated with principles of "plain language" use in government and legal communications. Plain language use in U.S. federal government administrative agency documents was mandated by executive order in 1998. Recent legislation, the Plain Writing Act of 2009 (Senate Bill 574) and the Plain Language Act of 2009 (House of Representatives Bill 946), extended the mandate.

Communicators who want to know more about plain language use might consult *Federal Plain Language Guidelines* (http://plainlanguage.gov/howto/guidelines/bigdoc/TOC.cfm). These guidelines are produced and frequently updated by the Plain Language Action and Information Network of U.S. (primarily federal) government employees. Links on this group's homepage (http://plainlanguage.gov) take you to resources for teaching, training, and learning. For a comprehensive list of resources, on the federal government website managers' guide Webcontent.gov, see especially "Writing for the Web/Plain Language" (http://www.usa. gov/webcontent/managing_content/writing_and_editing.shtml). For additional resources on the private sector, see the Center for Plain Language (http://www.centerforplainlanguage.org). For Canadian and global resources, see The Plain Language Association International (http://www.plainlanguagenetwork.org). For European Union and other national resources, see Clarity, an international organization of lawyers and interested lay people promoting plain legal language (http://www.clarity-international.net).

Accessibility is associated primarily with making website content available to users with physical impairments or difficulty in seeing, hearing, or making precise movements; individuals with limited English proficiency; elderly users, and others with special needs. Also, accessibility includes serving a broad range of visitors to websites. Many people in the United States and elsewhere do not use advanced capabilities of the technology because they have lower connection speed, screen resolution, or browser limitations. The cost of network connection time may be a limiting factor, too.

Writers who want to learn more about making Web content accessible might consult the following guidelines developed by government agencies and the Internet community:

- U.S. Department of Justice Civil Rights Division "Accessibility of State and Local Government Web sites to People with Disabilities" at http://www.ada.gov/websites2.htm
- United States Access Board "Electronic and Information Technology Accessibility Standards (Section 508)" at http://www.access-board.gov/sec508/standards.htm
- World Wide Web Consortium (W3C) "Web Content Accessibility Guidelines 1.0" at http://www.w3.org/TR/WAI-WEBCONTENT/wai-pageauth.html
- Federal Web Managers Council "Provide Access for People with Disabilities (Section 508)" on Webcontent.gov at http://www.usa.gov/webcontent

Summary and Looking Forward

From now on, public policy communicators' choice will likely be not whether to use the Web, but rather how to use it. Know-how involves judgment and skill. Discussion in this appendix informs judgment from historical and cultural perspectives. To develop needed skills, writers can learn by observing and practicing. Observe the variety of public policy websites. Practice recommended Web-writing techniques. Appendix B provides an opportunity for practice.

References

Allison, L., and M. F. Williams. 2008. "Government Websites" in *Writing for the government*, 153–202. New York: Pearson Longman.

U.S. House of Representatives. 111th Congress, 1st session. H.R. 946 *Plain Language Act of 2009*. ONLINE: http://thomas.loc.gov/cgi-bin/query/z?c111:H.R.946. Accessed 29 March 2009.

U.S. Senate. 111th Congress, 1st session. S. 574 *Plain Writing Act of 2009*. ONLINE: http://thomas.loc.gov/cgi-bin/query/z?c111:S.574. Accessed 29 March 2009.

APPENDIX

Clear Writing

Clarity occurs when readers easily understand the writer's intended meaning.

Problematic condition: Key information (main idea) is placed outside the key grammatical positions in a sentence (subject, verb, object) where readers traditionally expect to find it.

Problem this condition presents: Main idea is a mystery.

Causes of the problem: When the main idea is a mystery, it is usually because the sentence exhibits one or more of the following constructions typically used by writers with advanced education. That means you.

These constructions can displace the main idea of a sentence:

- nominalizing (rendering actions as static conditions; turning verbs into adjectives or abstract nouns)
- hedging (unnecessarily qualifying or modifying)
- burying the storyline (no identifiable actor or action, or too many)
- echoing (unnecessarily repeating words or ideas, usually close to the first use of the word or idea)

Problematic effects: Readers experience frustration or annoyance, and writers lose control over interpretation of content.

Solution: Writers should edit and revise text before readers see it. First, edit the text to identify sentences that need revision. Indicators: sentences exhibit the causes of unclarity shown above.

(Not all sentences will need revision; some will, usually.) Then, revise as needed according to principles and techniques described in the guidebooks by Williams (2007) and Lanham (2006) referenced here or in other guidebooks on plain writing.

Samples

Student public policy writers and an instructor permitted use of the samples shown below.

Acknowledgement

To the writers of these samples: Thanks for letting me use your unclear sentences for instructional purposes. From long experience, I know that writers learn best by analyzing their own writing. Made-up examples in textbooks can't teach you as well as your own writing can teach you.

What the originals show

Original sentences are shown as written. They illustrate the problem of concern, causes of unclarity. Generally, the original sentences are error-free. Error is not the problem here. Rather, style is the problem. Sentences exhibit problematically dense style that readers in academic work settings might accept but readers in a public policy work setting will not. Sentences like these originals will go unread in policy settings. There, readers want to get the point—who's doing what—easily and quickly.

What the revisions show

Revisions apply rewriting techniques presented in guides by Williams (2007) and Lanham (2006).

Revisions reflect a reader's attempt to understand the original sentence by asking "who's doing what?" Revision may have changed the writer's intended meaning. That's allowable in a demonstration, but not in real life. In real life, writers should self-edit. Don't let readers decide what you are trying to say. Don't force readers to work hard to figure it out. This demonstration prepares you to self-edit so that you can manage readers' interpretation of content and your intended meaning. Revisions shown here were written by students, either the original writer or a peer editor, or by the instructor.

Word counts are shown for both originals and revisions. Word counts are often reduced by half when sentences are revised for clarity using techniques illustrated here. Simultaneously, information becomes clear and concise.

What you can expect to gain from this demonstration

- You will learn to recognize typical causes of unclear writing.
- With sufficient practice in editing and rewriting for clarity, you will reform your writing habits.
- You will craft sentences that state your meaning plainly.

How to learn from these originals and revisions

Read the original sentence together with the revision. In the original sentence, pinpoint the elements that were changed in the revision. Do this by underlining words in the original that are omitted or rearranged in the revision. The first sample has been analyzed in this way.

To understand why those elements were targeted for revision, review the list of characteristic causes of unclarity (as shown above). Also, review the guides by Williams (2007) and Lanham (2006). Re-read those sources as often as necessary. Your objective is to learn principles and practices of clear sentence style.

Repeat those three kinds of diagnostic reading—comparison of original with revised sentences; analysis of the original sentence to find (and underline) elements altered by revision; review of guidance that explains why the changes were needed. Repeat until your editorial eye is trained. To achieve proficiency, practice editing and rewriting.

Revised for nominalization, hedging

Original. I would like to gain a working understanding of the method with which I should read, and possibly write public policy documents. (22 words)

Revision. I want to understand how to read and write policy documents. (11 words)

Revised for hedging, buried storyline, echo

Original. Having entered this country as a first generation immigrant, and subsequently earning US citizenship, I have had first hand knowledge of the immigration system, both its' virtues, and its' flaws. (30) But what I don't know is how to understand what leaders and politicians have to say, and how what they say can influence the public discourse. (26)

Revision. As a first generation immigrant and now US citizen, I know the immigration system's virtues and flaws. (17) But I don't understand public discourse or how leaders and politicians influence it. (16)

Revised for buried storyline, echo

Original. Many (probably most) nonprofit organizations are not concerned with public policy. (11) However, significant numbers of such groups do play a role in the policymaking process. (14) They typically play one of these roles: Either they advocate for a special interest or they perform analyses to inform policy choice. (22) Both types of information, advocacy and analysis, are useful for policy purposes. (12)

Revision. Many (probably most) nonprofit organizations are not concerned with public policy. (11) However, some are. (3) They either advocate for a special interest or perform analysis to inform policy choice. (14) Both are useful for policy making. (5)

Exercise

You can practice revising the following samples.

Original

1) I would have to say that thanks to my experience living abroad and immigrating has kept my views extremely open and so in relation to American policy and politics, I believe the American Immigration system has several advantages to it by it lets in highly-skilled individuals, however on the illegal immigrant issue, I do believe the U.S. can be a bit more lenient because

as Andrew has said that many of these people have fled their own countries because of economic hardships and persecution and I have to say if the U.S. continues on with this strict policy against illegal immigration that we may find ourselves lacking workers and our infrastructure may be severely harmed because of this. (118)

2) Diverse work experiences were worthwhile helping people in difficult positions and realizing the dilemmas of individuals in public services. (19)

3) I hope to learn how to communicate policy goals more clearly in an effort to thrive in a governmental affairs position. (21) I previously interned with the Town Inspection's Department, and was involved in tasks geared towards establishing specific goals to properly assess complaints and violations. (24)

References

Lanham, R. A. 2006. *The Longman guide to revising prose: a quick and easy method for turning good writing into great writing.* New York: Pearson Longman.

Williams, J. M. 2007. *Style: lessons in clarity and grace,* 9th ed. New York: Pearson Longman.

Index